The Vedic and Contemporary Holistic Health Approach for Lifestyle Disorders

aarogyaveda

CONCEPTUALIZED BY: **Ar. K. SHIVKUMAR**

An Evaluation of *"PST" Measures* *[Prevention, Screening & Treatment]*

notionpress
.com

INDIA • SINGAPORE • MALAYSIA

DISCLAIMER

This book provides general informational advice and is not intended to replace professional advice. The author and publisher disclaim any liability for any errors or omissions in the content.

Readers are advised to exercise caution when applying the suggestions, as individual circumstances vary. Before making significant lifestyle changes or adopting new health practices, it is strongly advised to consult with qualified professionals, such as healthcare practitioners or nutritionists, to ensure the recommendations are safe and suitable for their specific situation.

The author and publisher are not responsible for any misuse, misunderstanding, or misinterpretation of the content and are not liable for any consequences arising from their use.

The book also emphasizes the importance of a holistic health approach, which should be undertaken under the guidance of experts to maximize effectiveness and safety. Individuals with existing health conditions or those taking medication should consult with their healthcare providers before making significant changes to their lifestyle, diet, or health practices.

INTRODUCTION

My inclined interest and fundamental knowledge related to Holistic Health approaches accompanied with the hardcore experience related to safeguarding one's health during the on-going worldwide Covid-19 pandemic crises, enforced me to conceptualize the book 'SAPTAMSIDHI' dealing on varied Holistic Health approaches in sync with the Indian Vedic Culture and its impact and relevance in today's modern lifestyle. 'SAPTAMSIDHI'- being the principally conceptualized book, followed by other additional titles, **"AAROGYAVEDA"**, SANSKAARAM, PRANOYUGAM & SAPTAGYANAM.

"AAROGYAVEDA" being one among the other 4 more additional tiles of 'SAPTAMSIDHI, introduces the readers about **Modern Holistic Health Approaches**, which is **THE NEED OF THE HOUR** in our contemporary times of living and lifestyle disorders.

In the age of the internet, extroverted lifestyles, and quick satisfaction, these proactive guided exercises of **AYURVEDA – The Origin & AAROGYAM – The Trend**, both will aid in the development and enhancement of our physical, mental and emotional aspects through the **'PST Measures' – (Prevention, Screening & Treatment Measures).**

The most important aspect of **'PST' Measures** is maintaining good habits and a healthy lifestyle in accordance with nature by adopting our ancient Ayurvedic concepts in our day-to-day life, accompanied with the trending mandatory regular medical check-ups, early screening and diagnostic techniques which ensures to prevent a disorders/disease and assist to cure it.

While we cannot change our genetic makeup, we can still modify our lifestyle in quest of optimal health as prevention costs is always less than expensive medical interventions in the long run.

This book highlights ready-to-use tips that can help to prevent most of the trending lifestyle disorders. It also guides us for symptom prevention and lifestyle tips to manage our NCD's (Non-Communicable Diseases) / Chronic Diseases in the easiest possible methods.

AYURVEDA – THE ORIGIN

Our body constitution type, according to **AYURVEDA**, for maintaining an **OPTIMAL** healthy lifestyle throughout is being very smartly categorized in a tabulated format of **"TRIDOSHAS"** to clearly understand the readers and accordingly adopt the precautions and remedial measures to lead a healthy and peaceful life according to the natural transformations that occurs throughout the day 24x7.

Ancient Ayurveda wisdom teaches us to follow a daily schedule of eating, sleeping, digesting our food, working, and exercising in accordance with natural doshic rhythms in order to achieve optimal health and remain in ideal state of balance has been briefly explained in introductory topics on Ayurveda Clock, Ritucharya & Dincharya, Aahara & Vihara and Prakruti & Vikruti.

AAROGYAM – THE TREND

The Seven most common **LIFESTYLE DISORDERS** and its redressal through **THE 'PST' APPROACH** – (THE PREVENTION, SCREENING & TREATMENT) has been highlighted to the readers making aware about the Basic Symptoms, Causes, Effects, Prevention methods and the Diagnostic ranges of theses Lifestyle Disorders.

An evaluation awareness of **BEING-ON-ONESELF** has been guided to the health-conscious people by introducing ready reckoners, standard calculators and formulae related to the physical appearances, the diet in-takes and the optimal sleep requirement for a healthy and peaceful living.

FOREWORD

BANARAS HINDU UNIVERSITY
काशी हिन्दू विश्वविद्यालय

Established by The BANARAS HINDU UNIVERSITY ACT XVI of 1915

in BHU
प्रबंध शास्त्र संकाय
FACULTY OF MANAGEMENT STUDIES
INSTITUTE OF MANAGEMENT STUDIES

Date: 07-01-2024

FOREWORD

It gives me immense pleasure to know that **Architect K. Shivkumar** has conceptualised the book titled **"SAPTAMSIDHI"**– the Principle book which is followed by its other supplementary titles 'SANSKAARAM', 'PRANOYUGAM', 'AAROGYAVEDA'&'SAPTAGYANAM'.

The author has made a singular attempt in providing readers with a Reference Handbook for Wellness & Wellbeing that blends Ancient Practical Vedic Approaches for Today's Modern Lifestyle with advice on how to protect oneself from Modern Lifestyle Disorders through Prevention, Screening, and Treatment Measures.

Globally, there is an upsurge in psychiatric and lifestyle illnesses. I believe that these described and applied unique Vedic approaches and selected Yoga techniques such as Asanas, Pranayama, Mantras, Meditation, Mudras, and so on, when combined with the '7'- Seven different types of Holistic Health Approaches in sync with Indian Vedic culture, will provide a Holistic Treatment to cure these Modern Lifestyle Disorders miraculously.

This book's content will undoubtedly empower readers with a ready grasp of Hindu philosophy and profound information, helping them to live a healthier, happier, and stress-free life.

I truly think that **Architect K. Shivkumar's** book will be of great assistance to human society worldwide, and I applaud his efforts in creating an insightful and instructive work.

Prof. H. P. Mathur,
B.Tech. (IT-BHU), MMS, CAIIB, Ph.D.
Dean & Head,
Faculty of Management Studies, BHU.

Chairman, FMS/IM, BHU Placement Cell.
Director, Atal Incubation Centre, IM, BHU.
Director, Utkarsh Welfare Foundation.
Member, Board of Governors, UPES University.
Former Chief, University Employment Info & Guidance Bureau, BHU.
Former Coordinator, BHU Placement Coordination Cell.
Former Chairman, International Centre, BHU.

CONTENTS

AYURVEDA – THE ORIGIN

THE 'BMS' THERAPY
{The Body, Mind & Soul Therapy}

"स्वस्थस्य स्वास्थ्य रक्षणं, आतुरस्य विकार प्रशमनं।"

**Svāsthasya Svāsthya Rakṣaṇaṁ,
Āturasya Vikāra Praśamanaṁ.**

Ayurveda is such a scripture that tells human beings the ways to stay healthy, how to solve the diseases of mind and body.

1

INTRODUCTION

AYURVEDA is considered by many scholars to be the oldest healing science. In Sanskrit, Ayurveda means **"The Science of Life."** Ayurvedic knowledge originated in India more than 5,000 years ago and is often called the "Mother of All Healing."

The term *Ayurveda* is derived from the Sanskrit word *ayur* (life) and *veda* (science or knowledge). Thus, Ayurveda translates to *science of life*. It stems from the ancient Vedic culture and was taught for many thousands of years in an oral tradition from accomplished masters to their disciples.

It is a comprehensive approach to health and well-being that encompasses physical, mental, emotional, and spiritual aspects of life. Ayurveda's principles are rooted in a deep understanding of the interconnectedness between humans, nature, and the universe.

FUNDAMENTAL PRINCIPLES:

1. **Balance of Elements:** Ayurveda is based on the concept of the Panchabhootas, the five fundamental elements – Earth, Water, Fire, Air, and Space – that make up all living and non-living things in the universe.

2. **Three Doshas:** The human body and mind are governed by three Doshas – Vata (Air and Space), Pitta (Fire and

Water), and Kapha (Water and Earth). These Doshas determine an individual's constitution and play a role in their health and well-being.

3. **Personalized Approach:** Ayurveda recognizes that each individual is unique, and their health needs to be addressed based on their Dosha constitution (Prakriti), imbalances (Vikriti), age, environment, and lifestyle.

KEY CONCEPTS:

1. **Diet and Nutrition:** Ayurveda emphasizes the importance of proper nutrition for maintaining health. It provides guidelines for individualized diets based on one's Dosha constitution, the seasons, and the qualities of food.

2. **Lifestyle Practices:** Ayurveda recommends daily routines (Dinacharya) and seasonal routines (Ritucharya) that align with the natural cycles to promote balance and well-being.

3. **Herbal Medicine:** Ayurveda uses a wide range of herbs and natural substances to treat and prevent illnesses. These remedies are tailored to an individual's constitution and imbalances.

4. **Yoga and Meditation:** Practices like yoga, meditation, and pranayama (breath control) are integral to Ayurveda. They enhance physical and mental balance and promote spiritual growth.

5. **Detoxification and Cleansing:** Ayurveda employs techniques like Panchakarma to detoxify the body and remove accumulated toxins, restoring balance.

6. **Massage and Therapies:** Ayurvedic massages, such as Abhyanga, along with various therapies, promote relaxation, stimulate energy flow, and support overall health.

Relevance Today: Ayurveda is not just a system of medicine; it's a way of life that encourages balance, harmony, and self-awareness. While modern medicine focuses on treating symptoms, Ayurveda aims to address the root causes of imbalances. It continues to be relevant in today's world as people seek holistic approaches to health and well-being.

Holistic Approach: Ayurveda sees health as a state of balance among the body, mind, and spirit. It emphasizes preventive measures and personalized treatments to help individuals live in harmony with themselves and their environment.

Overall, Ayurveda offers a profound understanding of life and health that extends beyond the physical, addressing the interconnectedness of the individual with nature and the universe. It continues to inspire individuals to lead healthier, balanced lives and has influenced holistic health practices worldwide.

OUR CONSTITUTION & ITS INNER BALANCE:

Ayurveda places great emphasis on prevention and encourages the maintenance of health through close attention to balance in one's life, right thinking, diet, lifestyle and the use of herbs.

Each person has a particular pattern of energy—an individual combination of physical, mental and emotional characteristics

Energy is required to create movement so that fluids and nutrients get to the cells, enabling the body to function. Energy is also required to metabolize the nutrients in the cells, and is called for to lubricate and maintain the structure of the cell.

Vata is the energy of movement; pitta is the energy of digestion or metabolism and kapha, the energy of lubrication and structure. All people have the qualities of vata, pitta and kapha, but one is usually primary, one secondary and the third is usually least prominent.

The cause of disease in Ayurveda is viewed as a lack of proper cellular function due to an excess or deficiency of vata, pitta or kapha. Disease can also be caused by the presence of toxins.

In Ayurveda, body, mind and consciousness work together in maintaining balance. They are simply viewed as different facets of one's being.

To learn how to balance the body, mind and consciousness requires an understanding of how vata, pitta and kapha work together.

According to Ayurvedic philosophy the entire cosmos is an interplay of the energies of the five great elements—Space, Air, Fire, Water and Earth. Vata, pitta and kapha are combinations and permutations of these five elements that manifest as patterns present in all creation.

In the physical body, vata is the subtle energy of movement, pitta the energy of digestion and metabolism, and kapha the energy that forms the body's structure.

Vata is the subtle energy associated with movement — composed of Space and Air.

It governs breathing, blinking, muscle and tissue movement, pulsation of the heart, and all movements in the cytoplasm and cell membranes.

In balance – vata promotes creativity and flexibility.
Out of balance – vata produces fear and anxiety.

Pitta expresses the body's metabolic system — made up of Fire and Water.

It governs digestion, absorption, assimilation, nutrition, metabolism and body temperature.

In balance – pitta promotes understanding and intelligence.
Out of balance – pitta arouses anger, hatred and jealousy.

Kapha is the energy that forms the body's structure — bones, muscles, tendons — and provides the "glue" that holds the cells together, formed from Earth and Water.

Kapha supplies the water for all bodily parts and systems. It lubricates joints, moisturizes the skin, and maintains immunity.

In balance – kapha is expressed as love, calmness and forgiveness.
Out of balance – it leads to attachment, greed and envy.

Diet and lifestyle appropriate to one's individual constitution strengthen the body, mind and consciousness.

EVALUATION & TREATMENT OF IMBALANCES:

Ayurveda encompasses various techniques for assessing health.

The practitioner carefully evaluates key signs and symptoms of illness, especially in relation to the origin and cause of an imbalance. They also consider the patient's suitability for various treatments. The practitioner arrives at diagnosis through direct questioning, observation and a physical exam, as well as inference.

Basic techniques like taking the pulse, observing the tongue, eyes and physical form; and listening to the tone of the voice are employed during an assessment.

Palliative and cleansing measures, when appropriate, can be used to help eliminate an imbalance along with suggestions for eliminating or managing the causes of the imbalance.

Recommendations may include the implementation of lifestyle changes; starting and maintaining a suggested diet; and the use of herbs.

In some cases, participating in a cleansing program, called *'Panchakarma'*, is suggested to help the body rid itself of accumulated toxins to gain more benefit from the various suggested measures of treatment.

"Panchakarma" – Ayurveda offers one of the world's most comprehensive cleansing protocols, termed as *'Panchakarma'*. This ancient practice uses five primary therapies to release and eliminate accumulated toxins from deep within the tissues, and return the doshas to their proper seats in the body.

In summary, Ayurveda addresses all aspects of life — the body, mind and spirit. It recognizes that each of us is unique, each responds differently to the many aspects of life, each possesses different strengths and weaknesses.

Through insight, understanding and experience Ayurveda presents a vast wealth of information on the relationships between causes and their effects, both immediate and subtle, for each unique individual.

WHAT MAKES AYURVEDA UNIQUE?

a. **Holistic approach** – It looks at the whole of one's life. Health and disease are by-products of all aspects of one's life: nutrition, career, mental frame, social activities and spiritual life. If one area is weakened, all areas begin to suffer. If a person is unhappy at work or at home, it will affect all other areas of life. The five senses are the gateways that bring in these influences; what one sees, hears, smells, touches and tastes affects all areas of health and life. Life is like a web, if you shake one area of the web, the entire web shakes. Like that, what one does in one area of one's life affects all areas. Therefore, Ayurveda recommends that we take time to nurture all areas of life to maintain the whole (or holistic) balance.

 The state of mind plays a major role in how we act and react to the information and experiences gathered from the senses. When the mind is calm and clear, one handles a situation much better. The same situation, the same people or stresses exist at all times. How one deals with these situations will differ depending upon one's mental frame of mind.

b.   **Natural** – 'Natural' is today's buzzword but taking natural products is not the only way to a healthy life. The natural way of living is more important. Our body and mind are in constant communication with nature outside. In other words, nature outside is a reflection of the nature inside. Ayurveda helps us to maintain health by using the inherent principles of nature thereby bringing the individual back to one's true self. In earlier days, man lived in tune with nature's laws. The entire creation, the flora and fauna, follows the laws of nature and lives in harmony with it to maintain health.

c.   **Preventive health care and health promotion** – Ayurveda places great importance on prevention as it is far easier to maintain health than to restore it once it has broken down. Health is the state of harmonious chemical balance in a living organism. Our health depends on the chemical environments inside and outside our bodies. Food plays an important role in creating the internal chemical environment. Most of the time, having a diseases free body is considered as health. So, attending to the body in the state of illness is considered as sufficient measure for maintaining health. Routine discipline for body and mind actively strengthens immunity by providing a foundation upon which the treatment can build a new you.

Ayurveda describes the daily routine of human being from morning to night, a routine of self-control self-regulation and self-discipline, what to eat and what to do to maintain mental equanimity, how to live through the seasons of the year, by providing a biology presenting a fine prism of well-balanced diet, physical and mental activities.

These suggested disciplines of life called **Svastthavritta** have been classified into **Dinacharya (daily regimen)** and **Ritucharya (seasonal regimen)**. These also include specific food and habits to be followed and not to be followed with respect to health. **Sadvritta** explains the code and conduct for healthy living with respect to mental health. One who follows these three completely and continuously will never meet with disease.

The recalibration and changes in daily life like diet and routine in accordance with changing seasons has been astutely woven into popular culture in India through seasonal festivals and fasts by the ancient sages

The use of simple diet, nutrition, natural herbal supplements and periodic detoxification (panchakarma) helps to maintain health, rejuvenate and strengthen the body.

HEALTH DEFINED IN VEDIC CONCEPT & ITS INTERPRETATION:

- **Each individual is unique** – Ayurveda teaches us to understand our body; our particular nature; and our individual mixture of elements at a deep physical, mental and emotional level. With that knowledge we are able to identify activities, conditions, herbs and foods that either keep us healthy and in balance, or make us ill and throw us out of balance.

It recognizes the unique constitutional differences (Prakrti) of all individuals and therefore recommends different regimens for different types of people. Although two people may appear to have the same outward symptoms, their energetic constitutions may be very different and therefore call for very different remedies.

- **View of health** – Ayurveda defines health as a state of harmony of body, mind and soul. Disease free status of the body does not mean health. On the contrary, health is the harmonious existence and functioning of man in his body as a unit of the universe, a microcosm of the macrocosm.

Svastha, in Sanskrit, means 'a healthy individual'.

स्वस्मिन् स्थीयते इति स्वस्थः ।

Svasmin sthiyate iti svasthaha Sva – means Self and 'stha' means being established. Svastha means **one who is established in the self.**

समदोष समाग्निम्व समाधातुमलक्रिया।
प्रसन्नात्मेन्द्रियमनाः स्वस्थ इत्यभिधीयते ॥

Samadosa samagniśca samadhātumalakriyāḥ
Prasannātmendriyamanāḥ svastha ityabhidhiyate

A person is considered to be healthy when he is "having a balanced state of tridoṣas (three humors), agni (fire – the digestive power), dhātus (tissues), mala (biological waste products), cheerful state of ătmă (soul) and peaceful functioning of sensory organs and mind

Health or sickness depends on the presence or absence of a balanced state of the total body matrix including the balance between its different constituents.

रोगस्तु दोषर्वेषम्यं दोषसाम्यमरोगता ।
Rogastu dosavasamyam dosasamyamārogata

Imbalanced state of tridosas is sickness and the state of equilibrium of tridosas is health.

The state of equilibrium (dosa samyam) means a state in which the quantity, qualities and functions of the dosas are not affected.

विकारो धातुर्वेषम्यम् ।
Vikaro dhātu vaishamyam

When this equilibrium is disturbed, causing an imbalance, the quantity, qualities and functions of the dhatus is affected, giving rise to disease.

COMPLETE HEALTH

समदोषः समाग्रिश्च समधातुमलक्रियः।
प्रसन्नात्मेन्द्रियमनाः स्वस्थ इत्यभिधीयते ।।

Samadoshaha samaagnischa samadhaatumalakriyaha I
Prasannaatmendriyamanaaha swastha ityabhidheeyate II
Sushruta Samhita-Sutra Sthana – 15:41 (1500 BC)

Health is defined as the state of Balance of functional humors, metabolic fires, tissues and excretions with a pleasant soul, senses and mind.

ASTANGA AYURVEDA (THE EIGHT LIMBS OF AYURVEDA)

i.   **Käyacikitsä (Internal Medicine):** This deals with prevention, aetiology, prognosis and management of diseases.

ii. **Balacikitsă (Pediatrics):** This branch deals with prenatal and postnatal baby care. It also includes suggestions for the care of mother before conception, during pregnancy and after delivery of the baby.

iii. **Grahacikitsa (Psychiatry):** Deals with mental diseases and their treatment. It describes diet, herbs and other healing methods for improving the state of mind.

iv. **Urdhwanga cikitsa** (Ear, Nose, Throat and Eye diseases): The ayurvedic branch on Oto-rhinolaryngology and Opthalmology. Susruta Samhita and Astanga Hrdaya stipulate drug therapy of different types of conjunctivitis and glaucoma, along with surgical procedure of the removal of cataract.

v.   **Shalya Tantra (Surgery):** Deals with all the surgical conditions, involving correction of pathological conditions due to either external causes (such as foreign bodies) or internal causes such as ulcer or a dead fetus. The first recorded plastic surgery in medical history is described in Susruta Samhita. He has explained about the dissection of cadavers and the method to preserve them besides describing 101 kinds of blunt instruments (yantra) and 20 kinds of sharp instruments (shästra).

vi. **Agada Tantra (Toxicology):** Toxins can affect the body either through external cause like (snake bite or insect bites) or through food / medicine etc. This branch deals with management of such conditions and also with the toxicity and purification of herbs, minerals and animal products.

vii. **Rasayana (The Science of Rejuvenation):** This branch deals with sustenance of health and regaining youthfulness and promoting a healthy life. There are different types of rasayanas as Auṣadha Rasayana (drug based), Ahara Rasayana (dietary), Acara Rasayana (behavioural disciplines).

viii. **Vajikarana (The Science of Aphrodisiacs):** This branch deals with the means and suggestions for achieving healthy and intelligent progeny and promotion of virility.

Note: It is interesting to note that although these branches exist as independent fields of study, any condition arising in a patient is considered in a holistic manner.

2

BASIC PRINCIPLES OF AYURVEDA & THE PANCHBHUTAS

The following concepts and principles which are explained briefly simplify the understanding of Ayurveda.

i. **Sankhyadarśana** – Having base in darshanas (Indian Philosophy), Ayurveda deals with origin or creation of life. To understand Ayurveda, one needs to know the sankhya philosophy of manifestation and existence of universe.

ii. **Trigunas** – According to Vedic texts, all manifestations of nature – humans, animals, plants, consist of three primary qualities called guna. These three guna – Sattva, Rajas and Tamas – are subtle inner qualities that exist behind all material forms in nature.

iii. **Panchamahābhūtas** – The five gross elements are space, air, fire, water, and earth and the entire universe is governed by and composed of these five elements. Even these elements are not regarded as discreet quantities but are viewed as flowing into one another. Each includes in itself faint aspects of the other four. These five elements have an influence on everything in this universe. The element composition varies in each individual.

There is a balanced condensation of these elements in different proportions to suit the needs and requirements of different structures and functions of the body matrix and its parts. The growth and development of the body matrix depends on its nutrition, i.e.; on food. The food, in turn, is composed of the above five elements, which replenish or nourish the like elements of the body after the action of bio-fire (Agni). So, food, weather etc. have specific effect on our system depending on their element composition.

iv. **Tridosas** – Ayurveda describes three fundamental universal energies which regulate all natural processes on both the macrocosmic and microcosmic levels. These three universal energies are known as the **Tridosas – vata, pitta and kapha.** Though they cannot be seen they are known by their functions. Any procedure going on in nature contains three stages: **visarga (to give energy), adana (to take away energy) and chalana (movement).** Behind these three functions are sun, moon and wind. Similarly in our body the same energies are operating at the level of the human physiology continuously involved in all body processes.

v. **Prakrti (constitutional types)** – Every individual is a unique entity with a constitution of his/her own. This Prakrti or the biological judiciary controls the physical and mental faculties of an individual and remains constant throughout one's life. The Prakrti of an individual manifests as the physical attributes and physiological and psychological responses and is a result of the combination of gunas and doṣas in various proportions. A person in whom fire element dominates will show more personality traits of the pitta type, one in whom air element is predominant will have more vata traits and so on.

vi. **Agni (the biological fire of the body)** – Agni, meaning fire or heat has been given prime importance in Ayurveda from the point of view of health. The routine of daily life and the nutritional regimen, prescribed to keep this fire going has been woven like warp and woof in Indian life. This agni is different from the fire element in the Panchmahabhūtas.

vii. **Ama (toxins)** – In ayurvedic thinking, all diseased states arise as a result of ama, whether physical or mental and all ama is the result of an improperly functioning agni. Whenever the mind or the body goes out of rhythm with nature, ama begins accumulating in the system. Over time this ama causes physical distress in the form of disease.

viii. **Ojas** – Formed from the sap of all tissues, ojas is the ultimate refined product of all the food we eat. It connects one's physiology with consciousness and is responsible for greater immunity.

THE PANCHMAHABHUTAS IN AYURVEDA

Panchamahabhuta is defined in Ayurveda as the theory of five great elements of the universe for understanding the principles of nature's functioning.

Panchamahabhuta in Ayurveda are said to be in balance and the same thing applies to the human beings too. **Ayurveda** states that the human body is also made up of the 5 elements that are: **Earth**, **Water**, **Fire**, **Air** and **Space**. When these things occur within the body, the body suffers from sickness and diseases.

The 5 elements are seen in the body in the form of 3 body types known as '**Doshas**'. The doshas exist in all matter and are composed of different combinations of the 5 elements. They are: **Kapha**, **Pitta** and **Vata**. Their influence affects all mechanisms of the body.

According to Ayurveda, everything in life is composed of the Panchamahabhutas – **Akash (Space), Vayu (Air), Jal (Water), Agni (Fire) and Prithvi (Earth).** The Panchamahabhutas are described below;

Earth: Earth represents the solid state of matter and it indicates stability, permanence, and rigidity. The body parts such as bones, teeth and tissues are considered as earth element. Earth is considered a stable substance.

Water: Water represents the liquid state of matter and it indicates changes or unstable. Water is vital for the survival of all living things. The blood, lymph and other fluids are considered as water element. Large part of the human body is made up of water element. Water elements bring energy, carry away wastes, regulate body temperature and carry nutrients and oxygen.

Fire: Fire represents the form without substance and it has the power to transfer the state of any substance, for instance solids into liquids, to gas and back again. Fire element is an invisible energy that binds atoms together, converts food to energy or fat (stored energy), and creates nervous reaction, feelings, and even thought processes.

Air: Air represents the gaseous form and it indicates mobility and dynamic. Within the body, air (oxygen) is vital for all energy transfer reactions. Air is a key element needed for fire to burn.

Space: Space represents the space in which everything happens. This is the field which is simultaneously the source of all matter and the space it exists. The main characteristic of space is sound and it represents the entire spectrum of vibration.

Panchamahabhutas in Ayurveda therefore serve as the foundation of all diagnosis and treatment modalities in Ayurveda and has served as a most valuable theory for physicians to detect and treat illness of the body and mind successfully.

RELATION WITH TRIDOSHAS & GUNAS IN AYURVEDA WITH RESPECT TO PANCHAMAHABHUTAS

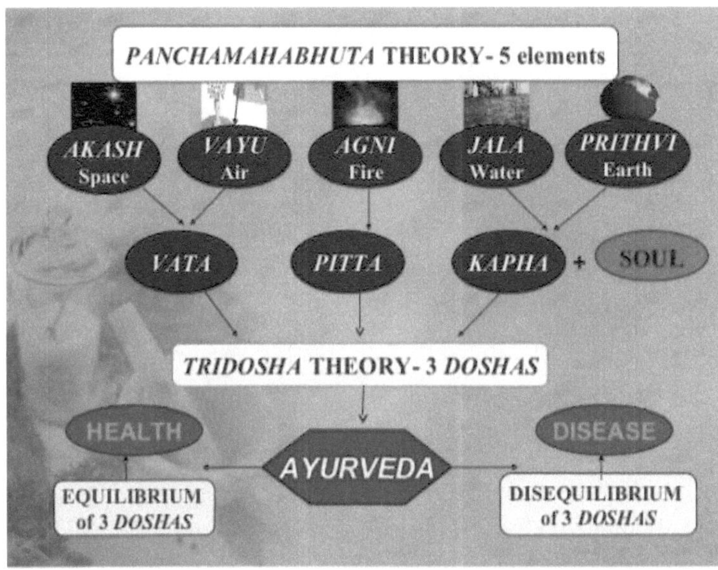

GUNAS in Ayurveda constitute three types: SATTVA, RAJAS and TAMAS. These principles interweave to create five elements.

Guna is the main principle of support within the material universe. These three gunas operate through five elements – the Panchamahabhutas.

TAMAS guna works closely with the physical functions of the body on the physical plane. It is summarized as doshas, tissues and wastes. It is believed that Tamas exercises great influence on the body's water aspect and gives the body its ability to consider and to bear long periods of growth.

Gunas in Ayurveda

RAJAS guna influences the psychic plane of existence and works closely with the psychological functions of the body. Rajas exercises the most influence on the body's air aspect, Vata Dosha (humour) on the physical level. This gives one the power to transform what is being perceived externally into thoughts, concepts, visions and dreams.

The third principle **SATTVA guna**, permeates each and every minute cell of human body. It functions through the existential states of awareness. However, it also influences the physical organism to some extent. It is believed that the sattva exercises the most influence on its fire aspect. The sattva also maintains the cosmic memory of the universe.

The three primordial forces: Sattva, Rajas & Tamas interweave to create the five elements or **Panchabmahahutas** which gives birth to the entire creation. According to Ayurveda everything is composed of the Panchamahabhutas

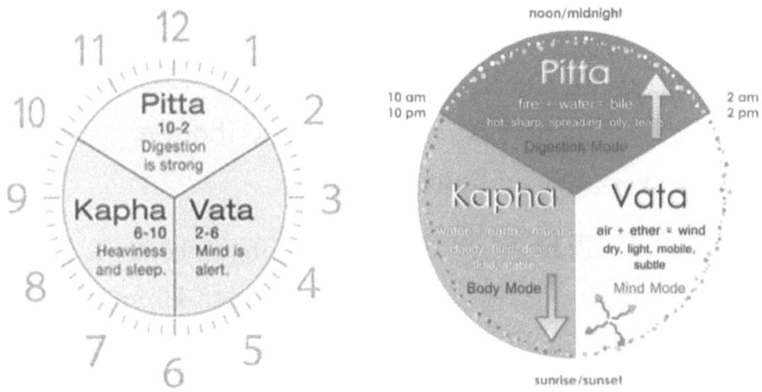

The Period & Duration of Vata, Pitta & Kapha Tridoshas & Its Elements, Nature & Status

Ancient Ayurveda wisdom teaches us to follow a daily schedule of eating, sleeping, digesting our food, working, and exercising in accordance with natural doshic rhythms in order to achieve optimal health.

WHAT IS AN AYURVEDIC CLOCK?

Ayurveda believes that there is an **'energy clock'**, that is, our levels of energy are in sync with time and there is an optimal time of day for different activities.

The concept of the Ayurvedic Clock is similar to that of the biological clock or body clock. It is linked to how our body and mind function relative to both the surrounding energy and the state of our bodily humors (doshas).

The closer our daily rhythms are aligned with the rhythm of nature, the closer we are to achieving mind-body balance and wellness. If we go against the natural cycle of nature, we experience imbalance and deterioration of our health.

HOW DOES THE DOSHA CLOCK WORK?

In the Ayurvedic Dosha Clock, the day is split into six 4-hour periods. Each period is related to a specific dosha and it is repeated twice in a 24 hour period.

- KAPHA TIME period – 6am to 10am & 6pm to 10pm
- PITTA TIME period – 10am to 2pm & 10pm to 2am
- VATA TIME period – 2am to 6am & 2pm to 6pm

- The rising (dawn) and falling (dusk) of the sun are connected to **KAPHA.**
- The peak of the day (midday) and the peak of the night (midnight) are related to **PITTA.**
- The transition between night and day and between dusk and dawn is related to **VATA.**

The activities we perform within these hours should be related to the respective dosha of that time.

By aligning our activities with the proper dosha we will be more efficient at whatever we do because we will be working within our own nature.

ACTIVITIES FOR VATA TIME

Vata dosha includes the elements of ether and air. **This time is the best time to access the ether and spiritual connections.**

MORNING 2 AM – 6 AM

- After 2 AM, our sleep gets lighter and our body starts to prepare itself for the elimination process.
- *Brahma muhurta*, 96 minutes before sunrise, is the best time to wake up. Brahma means knowledge and this is the time to seek knowledge.
- This is the auspicious and sacred time, the best time to meditate, visualize, and create.
- It is also the ideal time to go out for a walk and do yoga.

AFTERNOON 2 PM – 6 PM

This is a good time for communicating, socializing, and sharing creativity.

- Dusk is also another good time for meditation and exercise.
- Plan to have your last meal of the day before 6 PM.

ACTIVITIES FOR PITTA TIME

Pitta dosha includes the fire and water elements, and **Pitta time is the most productive part of the day.**

DAY 10 AM – 2 PM

- This is the time when our digestive fire starts to grow, and it peaks at 12 PM. The heaviest meal of the day should be taken in this window.
- Pitta time is for planning, taking action, and organizing.
- Schedule your most physical or analytical tasks during the Pitta daylight hours.

NIGHT 10 PM – 2 AM

- This is the time that we should spend in bed so that the body can repair itself. Ayurveda suggests going to bed before 10 PM. Levels of relaxing hormones such as serotonin and melatonin start to gradually fall from 10 PM onwards.
- This is the time when our mind is in a subconscious state, and when we experience colorful dreams.

ACTIVITIES FOR KAPHA TIME

Kapha dosha comprises earth and water elements. **Kapha nature is heavy and nourishment and Kapha time is a perfect time for self-care rituals.**

MORNING 6 AM – 10 AM

- We should be awake in the Kapha hours so as to draw prana (life force) into the body.
- Aim to complete elimination in the Kapha hour.
- It is time to move very slowly by performing gentle warming exercises.
- Have a light breakfast, gather energy for the day, and prepare your whole day's schedule at that time.

EVENING 6 PM – 10 PM

- This is the hour to slow down and assimilate your energy.
- It is a time that you should devote to your family and your loved ones.

- Prepare your body for it to go within (get grounded), and prepare to enter a rest and repair mode.
- A warm oil massage (Abhyanga) also adds to a feeling of heaviness that will relax your body and senses, and help you achieve deep rest.
- Turn off your screens and reach for a relaxing book before 9:00 PM at the latest.

Knowledge of this Ayurvedic routine has been around for thousands of years and it has been passed down through the sciences of yoga and Ayurveda.

However, our modern lifestyle has made it difficult for us to comply with natural rhythms. These rhythms are not rules invented by Ayurveda, they are the basic needs of our body and mind.

By understanding your dosha and how it functions, you can better understand how the energy around you affects your constitution and inner being.

4

TRIDOSHAS – VATA, PITTA & KAPHA

THE SEVEN CATEGORIES OF TRIDOSHAS

Depending upon the relative predominance of the three pathophysiological factors (dosha) the psychosomatic constitution of an individual may be divided into seven categories namely vata, pitta, kapha, vata-pitta, vata-kapha, pitta-kapha and samdosha.

The constitutional determination provides insight into the deeper workings of an individual. With this it is possible to become aware of the foods, spices, herbal medicines, emotions, thoughts, climates, colours, life-styles and so on that it tend to either balance or unbalance a particular individual and to either improve or aggravate various types of illness.

The constitution is considered to determine the susceptibility to different diseases, their progress, pattern, possible complications and the overall prognosis. It determines the individual's response to a particular therapy.

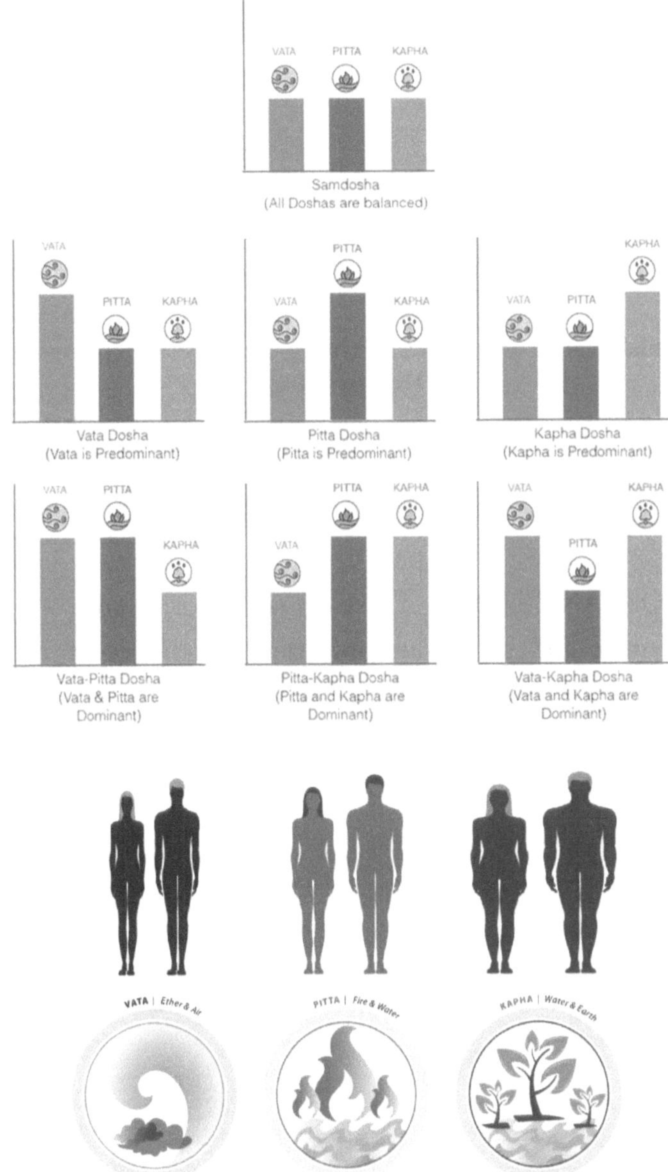

The Physical Body Composition as per the Tridoshas w.r.t Its Natural Elements

AYURVEDA CLOCK

[For a complete 24 hour schedule & this is divided in 6 zones of 4 hours each]

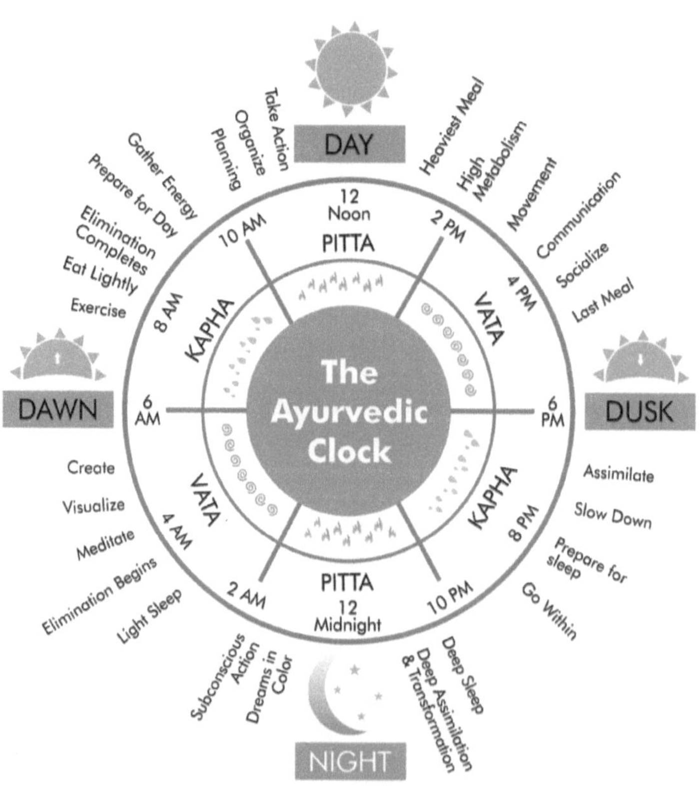

Sunshine Ayurveda | www.sunshineayurveda.com.au

An Ayurveda Clock/Energy Clock for an Optimal Time of the Day for Different Activities

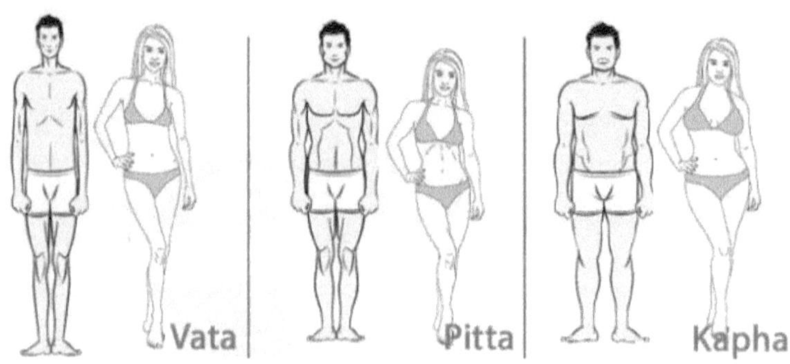

Visual Aspects of Tridosha Effects on the Physical Apperance of Human Beings

Compare the Tridosha Body Mind Type and Evaluate yourself what type of dosha do you have..........................

IMPORTANT NOTE: These visual pictorial images of an adult male and female are only for the purpose of visually indicating the physical stature of the human body, depicting the Effects of 'TRIDOSHAS' (Vata, Pitta & Kapha), on the Physical appearance of human body and how truly a person looks alike.

RELEVANCE OF THE BODY CONSTITUTION (PRAKRITI) – VATA, PITTA & KAPHA IN AYURVEDA

A skilled **Ayurvedic physician** can measure an individual's pulse and give information about the Individual's **'Prakriti' (constitution).**

The five elements Akash (Space), Vayu (Air), Jal (Water), Agni (Fire) and Prithvi (Earth) come together to create three basic constitutional types – the Vata, Pitta & Kapha.

The concept of body constitution, known as Vata, Pitta, and Kapha, is of utmost importance in Ayurveda. Understanding one's unique constitution helps individuals make informed choices about diet, lifestyle, and therapies that support their overall well-being. Here's the relevance of the body constitution (Prakriti) in Ayurveda:

1. **Personalized Approach:** Each person has a unique combination of Vata, Pitta, and Kapha, which determines their inherent physical, mental, and emotional characteristics. Recognizing this individuality allows Ayurveda to provide personalized recommendations for health and lifestyle.

2. **Disease Prevention:** When a person's constitution is in balance, they are less likely to fall ill. Ayurveda focuses on maintaining this equilibrium, helping prevent imbalances that could lead to diseases. By understanding their constitution, individuals can make choices that support their natural state of health.

3. **Treatment Strategy:** In Ayurveda, treatment is not one-size-fits-all. Ayurvedic practitioners consider a person's constitution when recommending therapies, diets, and herbal remedies. Treatments are tailored to address specific imbalances in the context of the individual's Prakriti.

4. **Diet and Nutrition:** Understanding one's constitution helps determine which foods are best suited for them. Different Doshas have different dietary needs. For example, a Pitta-dominant person may benefit from cooling foods, while a Vata-dominant person may require grounding and nourishing foods.

5. **Lifestyle Recommendations:** The daily routine and lifestyle practices vary based on one's Prakriti. Activities such as exercise, meditation, and sleep patterns are adjusted to support the individual's constitution.

6. **Identifying Imbalances:** Knowing one's constitution helps identify potential imbalances early. When an individual's natural balance is disrupted, it can lead to health issues. Recognizing the signs of Dosha imbalances helps in timely intervention.

7. **Emotional Well-being:** Ayurveda links the Doshas to psychological traits. Understanding the emotional tendencies associated with each Dosha can help individuals manage their emotions better and foster mental well-being.

8. **Mind-Body Connection:** The constitution affects both the physical and mental aspects of a person. Imbalances in the Doshas can manifest as physical symptoms or psychological issues. By addressing the constitution, Ayurveda aims to harmonize the mind and body.

9. **Holistic Approach:** Ayurveda's focus on individual constitution underscores its holistic nature. It doesn't just address symptoms; it considers the person as a whole. Balancing the Doshas promotes overall health and vitality.

10. **Self-awareness:** Understanding one's constitution cultivates self-awareness. Individuals learn to recognize their strengths, challenges, and tendencies. This self-awareness supports conscious decision-making in daily life.

In summary, the relevance of Vata, Pitta, and Kapha constitutions in Ayurveda lies in its ability to offer personalized guidance for health, well-being, and disease prevention. By embracing one's unique constitution and making lifestyle choices that align with it, individuals can experience enhanced vitality and harmony in their body, mind, and spirit.

The below tabulated format of VATA, PITTA & KAPHA offers more up-to-date choices in health care methods which are most appropriate for an individual.

4) *BODY CONSTITUTION (PRAKRITI) - CHART AS PER AYURVEDA - VATA, PITTA & KAPHA (DOSHAS)*

		1
SR.	**DESCRIPTION**	**VATA DOSHA**
1	**BASIC ELEMENTS**	AIR + ETHER
2	**TIME CLOCK – EFFECTIVE PERIOD**	2 AM TO 6 AM & 2 PM TO 6 PM Transition between NIGHT & DAY AND DUSK & DAWN
3	**PREFERBLY ALIGNED ACTIVITY**	**DAWN**: Mediatating & Waking up with clear mind & active body ensures to navigate throughout the day. **DUSK**: Creative Work & Calming activities physically & mentally during this transistion from Day to Night.
4	**FUNCTIONS –**	**Movement or Propulsion**
	i) AT BODILY LEVEL	Heartbeat, Blood flow, Neural currents
	ii) AT MIND LEVEL	Thinking process, Creativity, Agility
5	**CHARACTERISTIZED BY –**	**AIR** Element
	i) PROPERTIES	Cold, Light, Dry, Rough, Moving, Irregular and Changeable
	ii) NATURE	Wind, Oceans
6	**BENEFITS WHEN BALANCED**	Creative, Spiritual, Abstract thinking Sublest and most mobile of all the three energies.
7	**PROBLEMS WHEN IMBALANCED**	Weight loss, Insomnia, Brittle nails and dry skin. It upsets the overall balance in the constittutional build-up
8	**THINGS TO AVOID**	Wind, Caffeine, Travelling, Irregular routine, Irregular meals
9	**TO BALANCE WHAT TO BE DONE**	Be Moderate, Have adequate sleep, Follow disciplined schedule, Take sun bath, Avoid over work & stress, Feel the wind & cold
10	**PHYSICAL, MENTAL & EMOTIONAL –**	
	i) SATTVIC EFFECT TRAITS –	Creative, Inspired, Enthusiastic, Genuine, Artistic, Intutive, Divine, Love.

2	3
PITTA DOSHA	**KAPHA DOSHA**
FIRE + WATER	WATER + EARTH
10 AM TO 2 PM & 10 PM TO 2 AM Peak of MIDDAY & Peak of MIDNIGHT	6 AM TO 10 AM & 6 PM TO 10 PM The RISING (Dawn) & FALLING (Dusk) of the SUN
MIDDAY: Digestive, Metabolic & Productivity at peak. The largest meal of the day is advisable **MIDNIGHT**: Body is in active mode internally, setting up tasks for detoxification, cleansing and rejuvenation.	**RISING SUN:** Waking up in this period gives rise to heavier feeling in body & mind. Breakfast is advised to be light. **SETTING SUN:** Advisable to have light and an early dinner.
Transformation & Conversation	**Cooling & Preservation**
Digestion of food, Metabolic activities	Gives bodily structure, stability, lubrication & protection
Assimilation of knowledge, Intelligence	Healing aspect of body and its Immunity.
FIRE Element	**WATER** Element
Hot, Light, Intense, Penetrating, Pungent, Sharp and Acidic.	Heavy, Slow, Steady, Solid, Cold, Soft and Oily
Fire, Sun	Rock, Mountain, Moon, Earth
Intelligent, Focussed, Works tirelessly Good Metabolism	Strong, Trustworthy, Loving Stability & strength to body, Steady mind & good memory
Too hot, Ulcers, Skin irritations Digestive & Inflammatory disorders	Obesity, Lethargy, Congestion, Avoids exercise. Heaviness of body & mind
Heat, Alcohol, Smoking, Pressure, Stress	Cold, Damp, Oversleeping, Overeating, Heavy foods
Be Calm, Rest & Relax, Cut down striving, Avoid the sun, Stay cool	Be Active, Stay warm & active, Engage in stimulating activity, Avoid cold & damp things, Cultivate physical challenges.
Strong leader, Clear thinking, Spiritual Teacher, Perception.	Nuturing, Peacefull, Loving, Compassionate, Jolly, Generous, Patience.

		1
SR.	**DESCRIPTION**	**VATA DOSHA**
	ii) RAJASIC EFFECT TRAITS –	Nervous, Anxious, Manic, Hyper, Worrysome, Fearfull.
	iii) TAMASIC EFFECT TRAITS –	Depressed, Addicted, Psychological problems, Suicidal
11	**SEAT OF EXPRESSION IN THE BODY**	Colon (large intestine)
12	**PERSONALITY TRAITS**	Physicaly active, Busy, Hustling Anxious, Nervous, Fearful, Indecisive, Enthusiatic, Creative
13	**BODILY CHARACTERISTICS**	Usually low body weight & light bone structure
14	**SENSES**	Sound & Touch
15	**SIGNS OF AGGRAVATION**	Pains, Nervous disorders, Paralysis, Insomnia
16	**AGGRAVATED BY**	Prolonged & Intellectual Concentration, Late nights, Cold & dry
17	**PRONE TO ILLNESSES**	Arthritis, Anxiety, Infertility, Impotence, Digestive problems
18	**LIFESTYLE TO BALANCE**	Routine, Stability, Nourishment, Calmness
19	**FOOD GROUPS TO BALANCE**	Carbohydrates, Proteins, Spices & Fats
20	**TASTE TO BALANCE**	Sweet, Sour & Salty
21	**OILS TO BALANCE**	Castor oil, Almond oil, Gingelly oil
22	**AGE RELATED EFFECTS –**	
	i) PERIODICAL DOMINANCE OF DOSHAS	50 years & above – Eldery
	ii) IMPACT OF DOSHAS	Depletion in overall enery levels, Needs of body & mind become subtle & delicate.
	iii) COMMON AILMENTS	Depression, Dementia, Joint pains, Insomnia
23	**SEASONS**	Autumn – Sharad Ritu / Late Autumn – Hemantu Ritu Summer
	i) CLIMATE	Prefers Warm
	ii) DISLIKE WEATHER	Cold, Windy, Dry
24	**MENTAL & EMOTIONAL BEHAVIOUR –**	
	i) CREATIVITY	Full of ideas with poor follow-up
	ii) THINKING	Restless, Quick, Usually verbal

2	3
PITTA DOSHA	**KAPHA DOSHA**
Angry, Hot tempered, Judgemental, Resentful, Controlling, Jealous.	Attachment to things/object, Stubborn, Possessive, Holds grudges.
Voilent, Hateful, Vindictive, Hurtful, Murderers.	Intensly attached to pleasure & material things, Self loathing.
Small Intestine	Chest
Quick thinker with sharp tongue, Ambitious, Passionate, Often hungry & thirsty, Angry, Impatient, Intolerant	Calm and rarely irritated Slow actions & speech, Relaxed & Calm, Eat & Drink little.
Medium build with sharp features & muscular defination	Heavier build with large bones & some fat stores
Sight & Taste	Taste & Smell
Acidity, Skin problems, Heat sensitive & Burning sensation.	Anorexia, Laziness, Obesity, Mucous, Heaviness
Prolong & Intellectual Concentration, Hot & humid	Sedentary Lifestyle, Attachment, Cold & damp
High blood pressure, Stomach ulcer, Skin cancer, Heart attack	Cold & mucous congestion, Diabetes, Poor circulation etc.
Coolness, Relaxing in natural green, Devotional	Active, Smaller meals, Devotional
Leafy greens, Raw carbs, Protein, Cooling foods	Leafy greens, Spices, Fasting
Bitter, Sweet & Astringent	Pungent, Bitter & Astringent
Coconut oil, Sandalwood oil, Sunflower oil	Castor oil, Mustard oil
16 years to 50 years of age – Adulthood & Middle age	Birth to 16 years of age – Childhood & Adolescence
Assimilation of information & an increase in production	Growth, Nourishment & Building up of strength
Hyper-acidity & Inflammation	Cold, Cough & Allergies.
Spring – Vasanta Ritu / Winter – Shishira Ritu Rainy	Summer – Grishma Ritu / Monsoon – Varsha Ritu Winter
Prefers Cool	Enjoys seasons
Hot, Strong sun	Cool & Damp
Inventive with good follow-up	Best in the field of business
Organized, Accurate at optimal speed, Visual	Slow, Methodical, Uses feelings & emotions

SR.	DESCRIPTION	1 VATA DOSHA
	iii) MEMORY	Remember & forget quickly
	iv) MAKING DECISIONS	Anxious, Insecure, Tense, Unsure
	v) STRESS	Sigh & Hyperventilate
	vi) LOVE TO	Travelling, Art, Esoteric subjects
	vii) SEX DRIVE	Either in very high or very low gear / Variable
	a) FERTILITY	Poor
	viii) NATURE	Flexible, Optimistic, Lively, Intuitive, Enthusiatic, Changeable, Initiator
	ix) LIFESTYLE	Highly active
	x) SPENDING	Wastefull, Cannot save
	xi) SPEECH	Fast, Talktive, May ramble
	xii) VOICE	Weak, Low hoarse, Whiny
	xiii) EMOTIONS	Worry, Anxious, Moody / Fear
	xiv) SLEEP	Variable, Often poor, Deep if tired
	xv) STAMINA	poor, Over-exerts
25	**PHYSICAL TRAITS –**	
	i) PHYSICAL STRENGTH	Very active
	ii) BODY WEIGHT	Low
	iii) BODY FRAME	Thin, Tall
	iv) BODY JOINTS	Large Bony
	v) SKIN	Rough, Dry, Dark
	vi) HAIR	Dry, Rough, Grey
	vii) FACE	Long, thin with sunken cheeks
	viii) EYES	Small, Dry, Sunken
	ix) NOSE	long, Uneven
	x) LIPS	Dry, Cracked
	xi) NAILS	Dry, Brittle, Dark
26	**EXCRETIONAL TRAITS –**	
	i) APPETITE	Irregular
	ii) DIGESTION	Irregular with gas
	iii) ELIMINATION	Constipation
	iv) SWEATING	Less

2	3
PITTA DOSHA	**KAPHA DOSHA**
Average, Clear, Distict	Remember & forget slowly
Quick & Decisicve	Rather Inactive
Aggressive, Angry, Irritable	Lethargic, Dull, In-denial
Sports, Politics, Luxury	Calm, Complacent, Get anger slowly
Moderate, Passionate, Domineering / Often Intense	Constant or cyclic, Loyal & devoted / Steady
Medium	Good
Ambitious, Practical, Motivated, Sharp, Friendly, Courageous, Discriminating, Leader, Competitive, Goal-oriented	Calm, Peaceful, Solicitious, Resilient, Loyal, Slow, Deliberate, Relaxed, Caring, Stable, Nurturing, Patient.
Active, Intense	Slow, Steady
Moderate, Can save, Spend on luxuries	Thrifty, Collect wealth, Spend on food
Precise, Convincing, Purposefully	Slow, Monotone, Melodic, Cautious
Sharp, Loud, High pitched, Penetrating	Pleasant, Deep, Resonant
Angry, Irriated easily / Anger	Delibrate / Avoid confrontation
Medium, Sleeps easily, Rises easily	Good, Sleeps esaily, Difficult to rise
Medium, Can over-exert	Good, Under-exerts
Moderate	Slow, Sedentary
Medium	Large
Medium	Large, Short
Medium	Nicely covered joints
Oily, Smooth, Red	Soft, Pale, Whitish
Oily, Moist, Brown, Silky	Oily, Smooth, Thick, Curly
Medium	Round, Chubby cheeks
Sharp, Browm, Sensitive to Light	Large, Moist, White
Sharp, Pointed	Big, Round
Red, Moist	Pale, Moist, Big
Oily, Reddish pink	Smooth, Strong, White
Strong	Slow
Fast always hungry	Very slow
Loose	Moderate
Profuse with smell	Less

SR.	DESCRIPTION	1 VATA DOSHA
27	**EFFECTS OF FOOD & DIET ON DOSHAS –**	
	i) FRUITS which BALANCES doshas	Sweet fruits, Apricots, Avocado, Bananas, Berries, Cherries, Grapes, Lemons, Mangoes, Melons, Oranges, Papaya, Peaches, Pineapple, Plum
	ii) FRUITS which AGGREVATES doshas	Dried fruits, Apples, Cranberries, Pears, Pomegranate, Watermelon
	i) VEGETABLES which BALANCES	Cooked Vegetables, Asparagus, Beets, Carrots, Cucumber, Garlic, Green Beans, Okra (cooked), Onion (cooked), Sweet Potato, Raddish, Zucchini
	ii) VEGETABLES which AGGREVATES	Raw Vegetables, Broccoli, Brussels Sprouts, Cabbage, Cauliflower, Cellery, Eggplant, Mushroom,
	i) GRAINS which BALANCES doshas	Cooked Oats, Rice, Wheat
	ii) GRAINS which AGGREVATES doshas	Barley, Buckwheat, Corn, Millets, Rye, Dry Oats

2	3
PITTA DOSHA	**KAPHA DOSHA**
Sweet fruits, Apples, Avocado, Coconut, Figs, Mangoes, Melons, Pears, Pomegranate, Prunes, Raisins	Apples, Aprocots, Berries, Cherries, Mangoes, Peaches, Pears, Pomegranate, Prunes, Raisins
Sour fruits, Apricots, Berries, Bananas, Cherries, Cranberries, Grapes, Lemons, Oranges, Papaya, Peaches,	Sweet & Sour fruits, Avocado, Bananas, Coconut, Grapes, Lemons, Melons, Oranges, Papaya, Pineapple, Plums
Sweet & Bitter Vegetables, Asparagus, Broccoli, Sprout, Cabbage, Cucumber, Cauliflower, Celery, Green Beans, Leafy-Greens, Lettuce, Mushroom, Okra, Peas, Potatoes, Sprouts	Pungent & Bitter Vegetables, Asparagus, Beet, Broccoli, Cabbage, Carrot, cauliflower, Garlic, Leafy Vegetables, Okra, Peas, Peppers, Raddish, Spinach, Sprouts, Onions
Pungent Vegetables, Beet, Carrot, Eggplant, Garlic Onions, Radish, Spinach, Tomatoes	Sweet & Juicy Vegetables, Cucumber, Sweet Potato, Tomatoes, Zucchini
Barley, Basmati Rice, Cooked Oats, White Rice, Wheat	Barley, Basmati Rice, Corn, Dry Oats, Millet, Rye
Brown Rice, Buckwheat, Corn, Dry Oats, Millet, Rye	Brown Rice, Cooked Oats, White Rice, Wheat

The above chart is a detailed guide for our ACTIONS, AWARENESS, DIET AND SELF-CARE – TO CREATE BALANCE AND ASSIST IN GAINING MORE WELLNESS.

The Fast 5 Steps to Balance the Tridoshas During Its Effects

To balance Kapha	To balance Pitta	To balance Vata
Be active	Be Calm	Be moderate
Stay warm and active	Rest and relax	Adequate sleep
Engage in stimulating activities	Cut down striving	Disciplined schedule
Avoid cold and damp things	Avoid the sun	Take in sun
Cultivate physical challenges	Stay cool	Avoid: over work, stress, too much stimulation, wind and cold

5

RITUCHARYA & DINACHARYA

5) RITUCHARYA – AN AYURVEDA BASED SEASONAL RECOMMENDATION FOR WELLNESS & WELL-BEING

SR.	DESCRIPTION	1 HEMANTA – EARLY WINTER TO SISIRA – LATE WINTER	2 VASANTA – SPRING
1	**SEASONAL PERIOD**	HEMANTA: Mid Nov to Mid Jan: (Margshirsha & Pausha) SISIRA: Mid Jan to Mid March: (Magha & Phalguna)	Mid-March to Mid-May Chaitra & Baisakh
2	**ENVIROMENTAL CHANGES**	HEMANTA: Cold Winds & SISIRSA: Intense Sunlight	Hot Weather with Intense Sunlight
3	**BODILY CHANGES**	Digestive fire increases. Accumulation of Kapha dosha takes place leading to asthma, common cold, diabetes mellitus, Atherosclerosis	Reduced digestive fire resulting in aggrevation of the carried over many winter diseases. The accumulated kapha dosa also liquifies.
4	**RECOMMENDED SEASONAL DIET (AHARA)**	Eat Sour, salty, heavy, unctuous, thick meals. Use more by-products of sugar cane, gram/wheat flour. Drink milk & milk products, wine, rum, and hot water.	Old barley, wheat, rice, green gram & lentil to be consumed. Bitter, pungent & astringent taste foods which are light for digestion are to be consumed. Drinking liquids like honey mixed with water recommended.

3	4	5
GRISHMA – SUMMER	**VARSHA – RAINY SEASON**	**SHARAD – AUTUMN**
Mid May to Mid July Jyeshtha & Aashadha	Mid July to Mid September Shravan & Bhadrapada	Mid September to Mid November Aashvin & Kartika
Loss of Moisture & High Intense Sunlight	Rainy Clouds and Low Sunlight	Increase in Temperature and Sunlight
Reduced strength due to loss of moisture. Kapha balances and Vata starts accumulating.	Further reduction in digestive fire. All three doshas get vitiated in this season.	Weak digestive fire Pitta dosha starts vitiating
Sweet, Cooling, liquids and unctuous foods & drinks, ghee, milk, rice can be consumed. Drinking (fermented drinks-wine, rum, etc) should be taken in least quantity with food or by diluting in more water.	A general regimen consisting of keeping all doshas in Prakurta Awastha (Normalcy) should be followed. Use bit of honey in drinks and food. Food dominant in sour taste, salt should be consumed in cold morning hours to combat vitiated dosa.	Food dominant in sweet taste, light to digest, cooling, bitter taste properties bringing normalcy in Pitta dosha should be consumed in proper quantity. Rice, barley & wheat to be consumed.

SR.	DESCRIPTION	1 HEMANTA – EARLY WINTER TO SISIRA – LATE WINTER	2 VASANTA – SPRING
5	**RECOMMENDED LIFESTYLE (VIHARA)**	**ABHYANGA:** Application of oil to the whole body. Oil massage to the scalp. Warm clothes recommended. Staying in warm and less windy places.	Rubbing medicated dry powders over the body before bath. **Vamana therapy** – medicated vomiting exercise. Applying Kajal: Inner edge to outer edge of the lower eyelid. Sexual intercourse: once in 3 days to reduce Kapha dosha.
6	**TO BE AVOIDED**	Too much of Spicy (black pepper, capsicum etc), Bitter (bitter gourd, broccoli etc), Astringent (cauliflower, potato etc). Avoid sleeping during day time.	Eating sweet, sour, salty and oily food which is heavy for digestion and sleeping in the day time is to be avoided.

3	4	5
GRISHMA – SUMMER	**VARSHA – RAINY SEASON**	**SHARAD – AUTUMN**
During day time, one should stay in cold places or home & at night, sleep under moonlight. Wearing pearls, coral made jewellry at night and visiting cool forest areas and water bodies filled with flowers is recommended.	**Pragharsa Udvartana** – the act of rubbing dry medicated powder during bath. **Gandhamalya** – applying medicated drugs as a paste over body after bath are to be done daily during this season.	Favor practices that are calming and balancing, such as nadi shodana or gentle diaphragmatic breathing. Practice abhyanga several times in a week, using warm sesame oil-soothens nervous system & gives deep sleep
Salty, sour, pungent & hot food & drinks are to be taken less or avoided. More liquids are preferred in the form of juices. Exercise is best avoided in this season, as there is least strength in body.	Drinking cold juices, sleeping during day time, drinking river water, exposing to sunlight for a longer time and frequent sexual intercourse.	Exposure to sun rays when the sun is at its peak. Consuming meat of animals from marshy land, alkaline drinks or substances, curd, day time sleeping & exposure to winds are to be avoided.

DINACHARYA

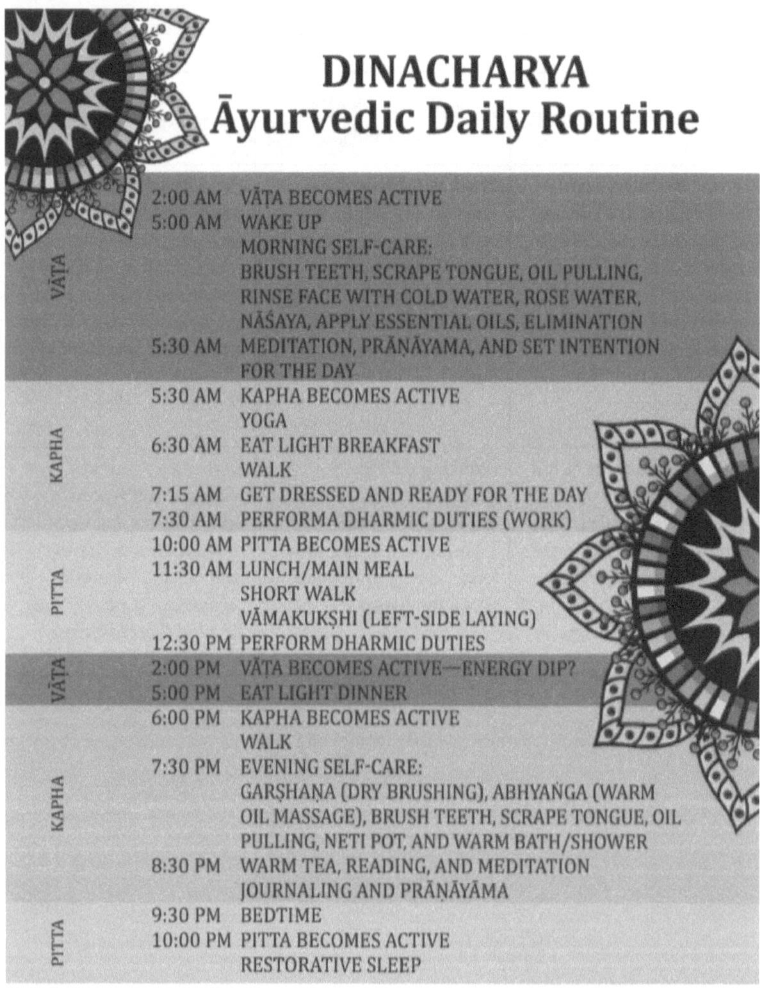

DINACHARYA
Āyurvedic Daily Routine

	Time	Activity
VĀTA	2:00 AM	VĀTA BECOMES ACTIVE
	5:00 AM	WAKE UP
		MORNING SELF-CARE:
		BRUSH TEETH, SCRAPE TONGUE, OIL PULLING, RINSE FACE WITH COLD WATER, ROSE WATER, NĀSAYA, APPLY ESSENTIAL OILS, ELIMINATION
	5:30 AM	MEDITATION, PRĀNĀYAMA, AND SET INTENTION FOR THE DAY
KAPHA	5:30 AM	KAPHA BECOMES ACTIVE
		YOGA
	6:30 AM	EAT LIGHT BREAKFAST
		WALK
	7:15 AM	GET DRESSED AND READY FOR THE DAY
	7:30 AM	PERFORMA DHARMIC DUTIES (WORK)
PITTA	10:00 AM	PITTA BECOMES ACTIVE
	11:30 AM	LUNCH/MAIN MEAL
		SHORT WALK
		VĀMAKUKSHI (LEFT-SIDE LAYING)
	12:30 PM	PERFORM DHARMIC DUTIES
VĀTA	2:00 PM	VĀTA BECOMES ACTIVE—ENERGY DIP?
	5:00 PM	EAT LIGHT DINNER
KAPHA	6:00 PM	KAPHA BECOMES ACTIVE
		WALK
	7:30 PM	EVENING SELF-CARE:
		GARSHANA (DRY BRUSHING), ABHYAṄGA (WARM OIL MASSAGE), BRUSH TEETH, SCRAPE TONGUE, OIL PULLING, NETI POT, AND WARM BATH/SHOWER
	8:30 PM	WARM TEA, READING, AND MEDITATION
		JOURNALING AND PRĀNĀYĀMA
PITTA	9:30 PM	BEDTIME
	10:00 PM	PITTA BECOMES ACTIVE
		RESTORATIVE SLEEP

art of living retreat center

artofliving.org | 800.392.6870

"DINACHARYA" TIPS TO OPTIMISE HEALTH AND RESTORE NATURAL RHYTHM

Dinacharya is a Sanskrit word made up of '*dina*' meaning day and '*acharya*' meaning activity. So *dinacharya* is a daily routine designed to maintain and connect us to our circadian rhythms or the internal body clock.

While Ayurveda has emphasized the importance of a connection with nature for millennia, western scientists are only now beginning to understand exactly how important it is for the body to stay connected to the rhythms of nature.

The disconnection from the circadian rhythms is called chronodisruption. It has been linked to a host of health concerns, including poor cognitive function, mood and sleep disorders, diabetes, obesity, daytime sleepiness, reduced school performance, substance abuse, heart disease, and some cancers.

Ayurveda tells us that on any given day, there are two cycles of change that exist – the sun cycle and the moon cycle – and they are connected with the Ayurvedic body type or *doshas (vata, pitta or kapha)*.

Dinacharya makes us understand the best time for our daily routine like waking, exercise, bathing, meditation, prayer, meals, study, work, relaxation, and sleeping. This is necessary to maintain a healthy body, mind, and soul.

BENEFITS OF DINACHARYA

- Helps in balancing doshas
- Helps in digestion
- Inculcates discipline
- Promotes peace, happiness, and longevity

DAILY DOSHA CYCLES ACCORDING TO AYURVEDA

First cycle (sunrise-sunset) – Sun cycle.
- 6 am to 10 am – *Kapha*
- 10 am to 2 am – *Pitta*
- 2 pm to 6 pm – *Vata*

Second cycle: (sunset-sunrise) – Moon cycle
- 6 pm to 10 pm – *Kapha*
- 10 pm to 2 am – *Pitta*
- 2 am to 6 am – *Vata*

Based on the above dosha cycles is a list of an ideal daily schedule that needs to be inculcated into our daily routine.

BASIC ROUTINE DINACHARYA

We live in a technology driven world where we get information about almost everything at our finger tips. We are well informed about the healthiest diet, best workout sessions and the easiest ways to de-stress. But in this fast-paced era, in our constant quest, we have lost the ability to stay in harmony with the laws of nature.

The divine and holistic science of Ayurveda has clear advices on how to stay in tune with nature by following a healthy daily routine. Make these Dinacharya rules recommended by Ayurveda, a part of your daily life and see how it can reveal the best in you.

MORNING WAKE-UP TIME (IN BRAHMA MUHURTA)

A healthy person should get up at Brahma Muhurta – two hours before sunrise. It is believed that the vata element is dominant during this time. Being the best time of the day, tuning our body into the frequency of the vibe's existent at that time refreshes and energizes us.

Start your day by waking up 2 hours before sunrise. This time called **"*Brahmamuhurtha*"** in Ayurveda is the best for any kind of learning. Your grasping power will be the highest during this time and yes, students benefit the maximum.

DETOX

Drinking around two glasses of warm water early in the morning helps in the detoxification process. It empties the colon and bladder and ensures healthy functioning. This will help in mitigating any chronic conditions of the digestive system that may arise.

Begin the day with a fresh start each morning by detoxifying your body mentally and physically. Cleanse your mind, fill it with positive thoughts and evacuate your bowel. Early morning evacuation of bowel is recommended in Ayurveda as waiting longer could lead to the build-up of body toxins called '*Ama*'.

MAINTAINING HYGIENE

Triphala or rose water can be used to clean the eyes. Our oral hygiene should consist of gargling the mouth with water, brushing the teeth and cleaning the tongue to activate the taste buds. Oil pulling or rinsing your mouth with coconut oil or sesame oil is recommended for healthy teeth and gums.

Wash your eyes, brush the teeth and do tongue scraping. Yes, even such minor things as tongue scraping have importance and are not exempted in Ayurveda. Traditional practices such as **Nasya** (nasal instillation of medications) and **Dhoomapana** (inhaling the smoke of medicinal herbs) are beneficial in cleansing the respiratory passages.

EXERCISE & BATH

Exercising is most optimal in the morning, between 6 am and 10 am because the body is in its *kapha* phase and at its strongest physically. It removes body sluggishness, ignites the digestive fire, burns fat and promotes the feeling of peace and joy.

Surya Namaskar, yoga and breathing exercises like pranayama will boost energy levels that will be beneficial throughout the day. Other alternatives are a brisk walk, a swim, or skipping.

Massage with medicated oil is called **Abhyanga**in Ayurveda. Doing self-abhyanga for few minutes daily before bath is recommended in Ayurveda as it imparts a natural glow and prevents premature ageing.

Energize oneself with physical exercise, yoga and breathing exercises. This allows daily rejuvenation of our body and mind and makes our body strong and flexible.

After exercising, a warm water shower or bath is recommended to wash away the sweat and grime. There is nothing more comforting than a lukewarm shower. But avoid using warm water, especially for the eyes and hair. Don light & comfortable clothes which feel good to the body.

PRAY & MEDITATE

Praying and worshipping is our time with God. It is also important to meditate for around 20 minutes to observe and balance of our **Prana**. This state is very important in *dinacharya* as this will bring in immense peace and contentment from within and set the tone for the day.

BREAKFAST:

Breakfast should be nutritious and wholesome. Eat a small amount, but make it big enough to get you through to lunch without needing a snack. Quantity may vary based on body type. Make sure the previous night's meal is digested well. Have a wholesome nutritious meal as this will lay the foundation for your day. Do not overeat.

Engage in your daily activities: With all the positive energy in your body and mind, start engaging in your daily activities, be it work, study or other duties.

LUNCH

Lunch is to be taken between 12 and 1 pm. The dominance of the *pitta* dosha makes it the ideal time to have the largest meal of the day. *Pitta* is responsible for digestion and it is advisable to stick to this time.

Ayurveda recommends that lunch should consist of wholesome food with all the six tastes – *madhura* (sweet), *amla* (acidic), *lavana* (salty), *katuka* (pungent), *tikta* (bitter) and *kashaya* (astringent). It is better to have a stroll after lunch to help digest the food.

Your *Agni*or-digestive fire is the strongest during this time and facilitates easy digestion

AVOID A NAP AFTER LUNCH

Anything more than a short nap should be avoided because it may trigger the accumulation of vitiated *kapha* which is not a healthy sign. A short nap, preferably on the left side, will keep you fresh and alert. Work or study can go on till supper.

For a nap after the lunch, Ayurveda says it can hamper your metabolism and increase fat deposition. You certainly do not want to punish your body by doing that. But yes, you may take a short nap during summer season.

TIME FOR SELF AFTER SUNSET:

Sundown is a special time of balance between day and night. This is the time for evening prayers and meditations in many cultures around the world.

This is the ideal time to relax after the hectic day. Experience the beauty of nature, offer evening prayers and detach yourself from all the stress and tension of a busy day.

DINNER TIME:

It should be taken around 6–7 pm. It should be lighter than lunch. A warm, light diet is preferred for a good night's sleep. Dinner should be at least 2–3 hours before bedtime as it gives the body ample time to digest the food.

This ensures optimum digestion of the food we eat and imparts sound sleep. Sleeping just after dinner with a heavy stomach may lead to a number of digestive problems.

Always take some time to walk for about ten minutes after dinner.

Time till bedtime can be spent with family and dear ones. Reading and relaxing can also be indulged in during this leisure time.

BEDTIME:

The best time to hit the bed is between 9 and 10 pm so that we can get 6 to 7 hours of sleep. It is advisable to massage the soles of our feet and head with oil before going to bed. This will calm the body systems and regulate well-being. Drinking Triphala before sleep will help in digestion, avoid constipation and keep the eyes healthy.

Fix your sleep time at around 10pm. Wind up all your activities, be thankful for the day and wish yourself peace. A sound sleep for about 6 to 8 hours is essential for an energetic and vibrant day that follows.

For the first few days, there may be some resistance from the body to accept this routine. However, if we make it a habit there is so much to gain as it's going to bring in peace, joy, and longevity.

Ayurveda is a way of living. There is nothing too complicated when it comes to taking care of our health. The above recommendations by Ayurveda can also be considered as preventive measures against lifestyle disorders.

RATRICHARYA

The regimen to be followed after sunset till morning falls under *Ratricharya.* According to our ancestors, the heavier or negative energies are at their peak at this time, hence we need to be careful and alert. Ahar, Nidra and Bramhacharya are the three sub-pillars of Ratricharya.

1. **Ahar (food):** Ahar should consist of light and easily digestible food. Avoid deep fried, cold foods, dairy products and sweets. A gentle walk after dinner is relaxing and one tends to feel light and mentally relaxed when going to bed.

2. **Nidra (sleep):** The hours of sleep as well as the time of sleep are important. According to the biological clock of the body, sleep during night is most beneficial. It rejuvenates the brain, makes us feel happy, nourishes the tissues of body, increases strength, pacifies tiredness and increases vitality. All this, in turn, increases the life span of a person.

3. **Bramhacharya (prohibition of sexual intercourse):** Sexual intercourse at the interval of three days in all seasons, but at the interval of fortnight in summer season is recommended by "Sushrut", (The first ancient Indian Physician, who wrote one of the world's earliest works on medicine and surgery and therefore regarded as the 'Father of Indian Medicine' and 'Father of Plastic Surgery').

6

AHARA & VIHARA

AHARA IN AYURVEDA

Ahara in Ayurveda is also referred to as the life supporting diet. It is actually the first pillar of Ayurveda and Ahara relates with the knowledge of proper diet. Ahara in Ayurveda is really critical as this science focuses on the strength of the person and not on the diseases.

Ahara is one of the three significant pillars of Ayurveda. It means that it is one of the basic principles upon which health, happiness and harmony along with the natural law rest. Ahara is concerned with diet and lifestyle and is fundamentally preventive in nature. Ahara is also known as the life-supporting diet is the first and foremost pillar of Ayurveda.

Ayurveda commonly refers to the knowledge of proper diet and it actually provides the first approach that can create and maintain ideal health and to alleviate the symptoms of illness.

Ayurveda emphasizes that while diet does not cure well-established diseases but sixty per cent of the illness can be controlled only by adjustments in diet and proper eating habits.

Ahara is defined as a real significant aspect of maintaining good and sound health. Ayurveda says that the eating habits should be conducive to health. So, it is very important to determine a diet that is most appropriate for the particular constitutional type.

Ayurvedic Nutrition understanding is quite different from that of the Western concept. The primary focus of the Western concept of nutrition is on the physical attributes of food, it means the amount of all the nutrients should be in equal proportion.

Ayurvedic Foods

On the other hand, Ahara is concerned with the effects of several types of food on the quality of the mind, balance of the doshas and the digestion.

Ayurveda says that almost all the diseases arise on the physical level from improper and inadequate metabolism system and it generally leads to weak and imbalanced functioning.

Ayurveda aptly recognizes the critical role that nutrition plays in the maintenance of mental sattva, which is the key to keeping the parts of life fully associated with their wholeness source.

In Ayurveda, it is mentioned that any food can have its maximum effect if all the five elements or the Panchabhutas are present in proportionate quantity.

Ayurveda use taste for determining which elements are in high amount in any particular food item. The basic tastes arise out of the various combinations and permutations of all the five elements. In some cases, certain tastes increase the influence of one dosha compared to the other and decrease the overall effects of the other doshas. Foods are categorized as per the tastes that pacify or decrease certain dosha's aggravation.

So, it is very important to understand the effect of tastes on the doshas, so that they can be kept in a balanced state creating optimum digestion.

In Ayurveda, it is also stated that the three doshas namely Vayu, Agni and Jala should be nourished properly and that can be accomplished by incorporating all the basic tastes in any food item. However, proper balance of tastes differs slightly from one individual to another. Maintenance of a natural equilibrium is very important in order to get the maximum result.

A proper balanced diet can correct present imbalances by pacifying the excessive doshas and strengthening the weak ones. It can bring back harmony in nature that is **Prakruti** – (constitution or nature, and consists of Tridoshas i.e. vata, pitta & kapha). There are several ways through which different foods affect both the quality of the mind and the body's ability to convert those particles into substances capable of nourishing the **Dhatus** – (It refers to the seven fundamental tissues that constitute the human body).

It is stated in Ayurveda that humankind is a part of nature. In the modern times, the ways in which the food is prepared and presented have changed drastically. As because of the rapid pace of life the trend towards urbanization, one can have less access to fresh food.

Today, the dependency on packaged and processed food has also increased tremendously. It definitely has some deleterious effect on both mental and physical health.

From the Ayurvedic perspective, it is very important to determine the proportionate balance of all the nutrients as it helps in finding out whether a food item is healthy or not.

The body has great difficulty in metabolizing the synthetic or inorganic substances in any food item. The body produces a toxic residue as a result of the synthetic or inorganic substances that prevents the nutritive substances from reaching the dhatus. Additionally, these harmful chemicals also damage the dhatus themselves. These responses actually strain the entire system and ultimately decrease the capability of the immune systems of the body to perform its functions.

Ayurveda calls the refrigerated foods or those foods which have been left overnight as lifeless food or **'paryushit'**. It defines that food that has been subjected to cold easily develops those heavy qualities that puts a strain on the digestive system of the body. It further impedes the metabolic process. However, Ayurveda is not against the principle of refrigeration that helps in preserving food. Another point related to chemically preserved food is that it has the added harmful influence of the synthetic chemicals, which is used to retard spoilage.

Ayurveda always gives emphasis on fresh foods. Raw foods should not be excluded from the diet completely. They should compose a quarter of the total food intake in a day. Another popular way of preparing food is frying. Oil in the food makes it difficult to digest and heavy. The deep-fried foods promote tamas in the mind because of the heaviness arising from the huge amount of oil that was used for cooking.

AHARA AND THE GUNAS

Sattvic Foods – Foods with a sattvic influence on the mind are usually light in terms of digestibility and they easily nourish the body and mind. Sattvic foods include milk, fresh foods, fresh fruits, ghee, grains, whole wheat, almonds and vegetables. These food items produce creativity, clarity, calmness and health in the body.

Rajasic Foods – Foods which amplify rajas in the mind actually increase the activity level and heat in the body. It includes garlic, onion, tomatoes, chillies, eggs, fish, spices, corn and radishes. These food items make the mind restless and emotionally aggressive.

Tamasic Foods – Tamasic food items are those food items that promote heaviness in the body. It includes fermented foods, cheese, mushrooms, alcohol, red meat, deep-fried fermented foods and especially leftovers. These food items not only cause mental dullness but also cause physical lethargy and confusion.

Ayurveda defines that human beings can do a great deal to improve the quality and prolong life by consuming a healthy Ahara and maintaining a good lifestyle. Ayurveda says that when appetite, digestion and elimination are normal the body has abundant energy. So, the concept of Ahara in Ayurveda plays a very significant role.

VIHARA IN AYURVEDA

Vihara in Ayurveda actually means the life supporting activities. This major principle of Ayurveda explains how to improve and maintain a healthy living standard. Vihara is defined as the second most important pillar of the **Ayurveda**. It means activity which highly influences the daily scheduled life that is full of **stress** and confusions. Just like the pillar of **Ahara**, this second pillar also plays a significant role in the proper functioning of the body.

PRINCIPLES OF VIHARA

The principle of Vihara or activity explains clearly how to act in different ways that are life supportive and it also includes lifestyle guidelines for maintaining optimum health and balance. In Ayurveda, it is defined that the successful use of Vihara's recommendations depends on the ability to know exactly what is good for the health and also on the motivation to act on whatever is known. The prime focus of the various lifestyle suggestions is to refine the quality of the mind.

AYURVEDIC ACTIVITIES IN VIHARA

There are actually an endless number of demands from various spheres and a lot of attention is required for keeping the minds constantly active. Additionally, the negative influences from the environment create confusion and fear. These negative influences cause the mind to be confined to a separate superficial level, where it is either too dull or too scattered to even experience the emotional, mental and physical resources that lay hidden most of the time. Ayurvedic scientists say that the limitless possibilities that exist in the subtler levels of awareness remain inaccessible except to a peaceful and settled mind. When the mind is strongly influenced by the **Sattva**, it is quite possible to have the access to such a calm and composed mind. This stage allows appreciating the whole of life and its various aspects.

Meditation is defined as the best way to enhance the quality of sattva and its positive effects. In Ayurveda, the first recommendation of Vihara is daily routine practice of meditation. Throughout the **history of Ayurveda**, each and every great civilization has endorsed regular practice of meditation as a way to enhance various aspects of life. Vihara in Ayurveda says that meditation allows one to transcend the active phases of the mind. It significantly restores balance in life and psychological health. Apart from meditation, another aspect of Vihara in Ayurveda is staying rested. This key feature promotes sattva in mind. One of the major contributors to the mind's loss of knowledge and knowingness is fatigue. With the increasing demands of the modern life, loss of rest and fatigue is experienced by almost everyone. Ayurveda gives tremendous emphasis on meditation and proper rest in order to promote health. These aspects allow the body and mind to release toxins and stress. Moreover, Vihara also suggests working in moderation. Getting exhausted negates the ability to enjoy the achievements.

It is a proven fact that desires are easily fulfilled when they are created from comprehensive and clear sattvic mind.

Vihara also emphasizes on **Exercise** for enhancing the quality of the lives of the people. Exercise helps in gaining energy. It gives importance to two types of exercise mainly aerobic or cardiovascular exercise and secondly sensory exercise. The first type of exercise strengthens and improves the circulatory system of the heart. The sensory exercise, unlike the aerobic exercise, is done in a very slow and gentle manner. It powerfully influences the mind. The recommendations made by Vihara for the daily routine life are popularly known as **"Dinacharya" in Ayurveda.**

Thus, Vihara in Ayurveda are designed to promote the body's normal and healthy functioning.

7

PRAKRUTI & VIKRUTI

PRAKRUTI

Prakruti or Constitution is the particular arrangement of energies present at birth is known in **Ayurveda**. Its utilization is up to us. It is the sourcebook for our health, strength and well-being and can also be the facilitator toward difficulties. Humans are far more complex and remarkable than any standard description could convey, whether it be Ayurvedic, Astrological, Biochemical or Psychological.

PULSE IN PRAKRUTI

A skilled **Ayurvedic physician** can measure an individual's pulse and give information about the individual's 'prakruti' (constitution). From pulse examination he or she can discover what **elements** are in balance and what needs to be done. The pulse is utilized in Ayurveda in a way similar to Tibetan or Chinese medicine.

ELEMENTS IN CREATING PRAKRUTI

Each constitution has different needs. All these needs assure the balance and better chances for good health and peace of mind. It also offers more up to date choices in health care methods which are most appropriate for an individual. The five elements Akash (Space), Vayu (Air), Jal (Water), Agni

(Fire) and Prithvi (Earth) come together to create three basic constitutional types – the Vata, Pitta & Kapha.

CHARACTERISTICS OF ELEMENTS OF CONSTITUTION OR PRAKRUTI

If air and ether dominate in an individual constitution, then the **individual is 'Vata'** in nature. If fire and water take the lead in an individual's physical form, than the **individual is 'Pitta'** in nature. If water and earth hold superiority in an individual's body from birth, than the **individual is 'Kapha'** in nature. 'Pittas' have sharp minds, passionate feelings (sometimes submerged) and are likely to want to lead. 'Kaphas' are solid, reliable, easy-going people, who shouldn't be pushed too far. Traditionally, the infuriated 'Kapha' is compared to an enraged bull about to charge.

'Vatas' go for warm climes, 'Pittas' for cooler ones and 'Kaphas' for anything but humidity.

Many people are born with double constitutions, or two **'doshas'**. A 'Pitta-Kapha' individual includes the characteristics of both these types and similarly the other duo constitutions.

IMPORTANCE OF CONSTITUTION OR PRAKRUTI

If an individual exploit his or her constitution and natural needs, he or she can become imbalanced. This imbalance or **disease** state is known as **'Vikruti'**. This imbalance can show up in his or her constitutional 'dosha'. If an individual whose original constitution (prakruti) is 'Kapha', but he or she has developed an imbalance in 'Vata dosha' due to his or her lifestyle choices. This 'Vata' imbalance would be known as his or her **'Vikruti'**.

VIKRUTI

Vikruti in Ayurveda means out of nature. It means the major imbalances of the body that occurs when there is certain predominance of any of the doshas. The innate doshic predominance remains hidden underneath the imbalances that are caused by the years of poorly maintained lifestyle and behaviour.

Vikruti in Ayurveda refers to the imbalances of the body. It is the inborn doshic structures that often distorted or obscured by certain imbalances. It is stated in Ayurveda that excessive functioning of the strongest dosha constitutes the most common cause of the imbalances of the body.

When a specific dosha is prominent it does not take much environmental motivation to aggravate it. In simple terms, the imbalance that obscures the natural and optimum relationship of the doshas is known as Vikruti. Predominance of any of the doshas in ayurveda that is not natural to the body's constitution will cause in the occurrence of Vikruti.

When this type of improper relationship exists among the doshas, **Aama** starts to form, damages the dhatus and impairs elimination of the malas.

Vikruti in Ayurveda is defined as a condition that arises from an incorrect relationship with the environment. Knowledge of this imbalance is very important as without knowing what is best for the body's particular system, exposure to harmful inputs such as inappropriate sensory stimuli, stressful activities and improper food is likely to take place.

Lack of proper knowledge about Vikruti may also lead to wrong or inadequate adjustments to the impact of seasonal changes. Such influences cause mental, emotional and physical stress, which overwhelm the normal system of the body, causing optimum dynamic relationship among the doshas to get distorted. This phase then compromises with the body's ability to adapt efficiently to the various circumstances of life.

Ayurveda stresses on the fact that knowing Vikruti is more beneficial comparatively. It is important for correct addressing of the imbalances of the body that cover the natural constitution. It is suggested in Ayurveda to select those food items that compensate for the constitutional tendencies towards doshic excess. Each and every Vikruti responds positively to a particular diet. Vikruti pacifying diets include grains, green leafy vegetables, and loads of legumes, dairy products, fruits, nuts, certain specific spices and oils.

Kapha dosha gives the moistening secretions and cohesiveness that nourish the body. So, when kapha dominates the constitution, a person gains weight very easily. People with kaphic constitutions have slow metabolism that take longer to digest the food. When kapha vikruti develops in the body all the favourable qualities get distorted. At that phase an individual becomes lethargic, dull and apathetic. People with kaphic vikruti are more prone to respiratory diseases and sinus associated diseases, obesity, indigestion and allergies.

In the body, when Pitta becomes excessive it generally shows the signs of anger, irritability, frustration and impatience. People with pitta dominant vikruti are more prone to emotional sensitivity and confusion. Pitta vikruti is also prone to acidic disorders, headaches, liver and gall bladder problems.

Lastly, people with excessive Vata dosha experience loss of concentration and restlessness. These people are more prone to anxiety, confusion and worry. All the psychological, neurological and degenerative problems are associated with Vata dominant Vikruti.

AAROGYAM – THE TREND

The "WELLNESS" Mantra
The Concept of "PST" Approach
[Prevention, Screening and Treatment]

स्वास्थ्यरक्षणं प्रथमं सुखानि, स्वास्थ्यनिरीक्षणं द्वितीयमेव च।
आरोग्यचिकित्सा तृतीयमुत्तमं, लक्ष्यं सर्वजीवानां सुखं च
दुःखारम्॥

Svāsthyarakṣaṇaṁ Prathamaṁ Sukhaṇi,

Svāsthyanirīkṣaṇaṁ Dvitīyameva ca।

Ārogyacikitsā Tritīyamuttamaṁ, Lakṣyaṁ

Sarvajīvānāṁ Sukhaṁ ca Duḥkhāram॥

"Preservation of health is foremost happiness, and examination of health is second. Treatment of illness is the best of all, the aim of all living beings, both happiness and relief from suffering."

HOLISTIC HEALTH – AN INTRODUCTION

HOLISTIC MEDICINE FOR HOLISTIC HEALTH

Holistic Medicine is a form of healing that considers the whole person – body, mind, spirit, and emotions – in the quest for optimal health and wellness. According to the holistic medicine philosophy, one can achieve optimal health – the primary goal of holistic medicine practice by gaining proper balance in life.

Holistic medicine practitioners believe that the whole person is made up of interdependent parts and if one part is not working properly, all the other parts will be affected. In this way, if people have imbalances (physical, emotional, or spiritual) in their lives, it can negatively affect their overall health.

A holistic doctor may use all forms of health care, from conventional medication to alternative therapies, to treat a patient. For example, when a person suffering from migraine headaches pays a visit to a holistic doctor, instead of walking out solely with medications, the doctor will likely take a look at all the potential factors that may be causing the person's headaches, such as other health problems, diet and sleep habits, stress and personal problems, and preferred spiritual practices. The treatment plan may involve drugs to relieve symptoms, but also lifestyle modifications to help prevent the headaches from recurring.

PRINCIPLES OF HOLISTIC MEDICINE

Holistic medicine is based on the belief that unconditional love and support is the most powerful healer and a person is ultimately responsible for his or her own health and well-being. Other principles of holistic medicine include the following:

- All people have innate healing powers.
- The patient is a person, not a disease.
- Healing takes a team approach involving the patient and doctor, and addresses all aspects of a person's life using a variety of health care practices.
- Treatment involves fixing the cause of the condition, not just alleviating the symptoms.

HOLISTIC MEDICINE: TYPES OF TREATMENTS

Holistic practitioners use a variety of treatment techniques to help their patients take responsibility for their own well-being and achieve optimal health. Depending on the practitioner's training, these may include:

- Patient education on lifestyle changes and self-care to promote wellness. This may include diet, exercise, psychotherapy, relationship and spiritual counselling, and more
- Complementary and alternative therapies such as ayurveda, homeopathy, acupuncture, massage therapy, naturopathy, yogic kriyas and others.
- Western medications and surgical procedures

This Holistic theory is applicable to the four interrelated dimensional parts:

1. PHYSICAL
2. MENTAL
3. EMOTIONAL
4. SPIRITUAL

These parts of a human being work cohesively together in order to facilitate homeostatic, well-being for optimal health.

HOLISTIC HEALTH

Holistic Health is actually an approach to life. Rather than focusing on illness or specific parts of the body, this ancient approach to **health** considers the whole person and how he or she interacts with his or her environment. It emphasizes the connection of mind, body and spirit.

Holism is the theory that the parts of any whole cannot exist and cannot be understood except in their relation to the whole; "holism holds that the whole is greater than the sum of its parts"; that parts of a whole are in intimate interconnection, such that they cannot exist or be understood independently of the whole. The principles of holism have been around since the time of Hippocrates, 2500 years ago and even earlier then the eastern healing traditions of Ayurvedic and traditional Chinese medicine.

1) DEFINATION OF HOLISTIC HEALTH

The definition of holistic health includes a balanced approach of healing the mind, body and spirit.

2) CONCEPT OF HOLISTIC HEALTH

When it concerns holistic health, there are several basic concepts that are widely followed and practised.

a. Finding the root causes of the diseases or symptoms.
b. Removing the underlying causes.
c. Purifying the body of toxins and infections.
d. Restoring nutrient deficiencies to allow the body to heal and restore health.

3) THE IMPORTANCE OF HOLISTIC HEALTH

While people are living longer today they also are experiencing chronically high levels of stress and fatigue, are consuming nutrient depleted foods, and are exposed to hundreds of potentially harmful chemicals through air, water, cleaning, and personal care products daily. So to say that holistic health is important would be an understatement.

For many living with chronic disease and undiagnosable symptoms, the modern-day healthcare industry has failed them, and it is time that a more holistic, whole-body solution became a standard part of the way we treat and support the health of the billions of people living on this planet.

Holistic health also takes into account the many external and environmental factors which could be supporting or impacting our overall health and wellness, and with climate change impacting our surrounding environments more and more each day, it is important that we have a systematic way of addressing health in the future.

4) THE 5 ASPECTS OF HOLISTIC HEALTH: PHYSICAL, MENTAL, EMOTIONAL, SPIRITUAL & SOCIAL

When it comes to holistic health we are looking beyond the physical body and are addressing physical, mental, emotional, spiritual and social aspects.

All of these 5 aspects of holistic health are what enable a person to truly live each day in the healthiest, happiest way possible and if one area if compromised, most likely other areas will be as well.

I) PHYSICAL

Our physical health is what most people think about when they think of health. This is mostly because it is the physical body that often shows us physical signs and symptoms of either optimal or sub-optimal health. These physical signs and symptoms are easier to track and measure, versus other non-physical signs and symptoms that can feel more abstract.

When it comes to supporting our physical health there are few key practices that everyone can benefit from and can make a huge difference on our overall well-being.

Ways that we can support our physical health:

- Sleep for 8 hours each night. This will allow our body to truly rest and repair from the day.
- Eat a nutrient dense diet that is high in plant-based foods and organic/pastured animal products.
- Maintain a balanced blood sugar by eating meals and snacks that contain fat, carbohydrates, and protein every 3-4 hours.
- Movement of our body for 30 minutes each day is compulsory. While every person's exercise routine will be different, everyone can benefit from at least 30 minutes of movement each day.
- Limit processed foods and hydrogenated oils which are highly inflammatory and can increase risk to chronic disease.
- Do no smoke, and avoid excessive alcohol consumption.

II) MENTAL

The next aspect of holistic health is our mental health, which often overlaps with both our emotional and physical health. The big distinction between our mental and emotional health is that, while our emotional health refers mostly to our daily mood and emotions, our mental health refers to our cognitive abilities that affect how our brain functions.

Ways that we can support our mental health:

- Always keep our mind active by seeking out learning opportunities and problem-solving practices that challenge our brain.
- Consume nutrient dense foods that are high in antioxidants and omega-3 fatty acids that will help to reduce overall inflammation and support cognitive function.
- Avoid excessive drinking, smoking, and consuming recreational drugs.
- Improve gut health with gut healing foods like prebiotic and probiotic rich foods. Since the brain is directly connected to the gut a healthy gut is essential for a healthy mind.

III) EMOTIONAL

While often overlooked, our emotional health is just as important as our physical health — especially because our emotional health can affect our physical health if it is not prioritized.

Ways we can support our emotional health:

- Seek out therapy when needed. Therapy is an essential part of supporting our emotional health and should be utilized whenever necessary.

- Practice mindfulness and stress reduction habits that can help us better manage life's daily stressors.
- Keep a journal to record our thoughts and feelings. Use the journal to record what we are grateful for as it can help bring positivity into times of stress.

IV) SPIRITUAL

Spiritual wellness does not necessarily mean that we need to become religious, although the two often have overlapping practices and principles. Instead, our spiritual health should focus on how we are connecting with our inner soul, and the greater world around us.

Ways we can support our spiritual health:

- Spend time in nature
- Spend a few minutes each day meditating
- If we are religious, take the time to practice our faith

V) SOCIAL

Research has shown that the happiest people on earth have deep connections with their friends, family, and community. This is often why religion is connected with happiness as it can provide a deep sense of community and support, no matter what faith a person chooses.

Ways that we can support our social health:

- Make time for in-person connection. While technology has allowed for us to feel connected more, research has shown that virtual connection still does not provide us with the same level of happiness as in-person connection does.

- Get involved in your local community. Whether this is through our religion related approaches and moves, local volunteer organizations, clubs, or programs at your kid school — getting involved in your local community is one of the best ways we can support our social health and improve happiness.

- Set boundaries with people in your life that may increase stress or bring about toxic energy. Also do not be afraid to walk away from friendships and relationships that are negatively affecting your health.

LIFESTYLE DISORDERS

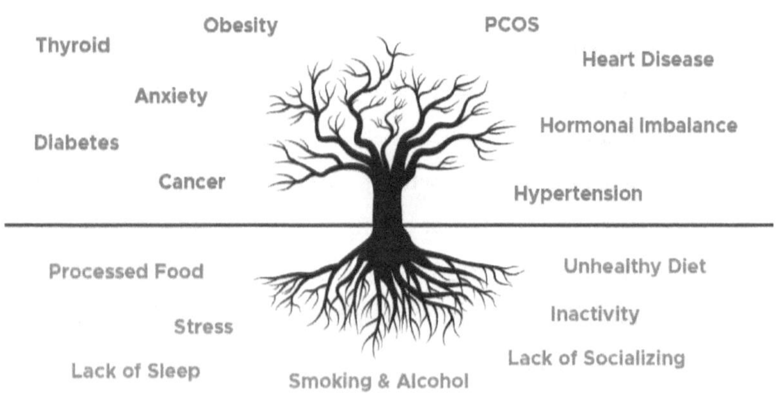

The Growing Roots of Lifestyle Disorders

NON COMMUNICABLE DISEASES (NCD's)

Non-Communicable Diseases (NCDs), also known as chronic diseases, are a group of medical conditions that are not primarily caused by infections and are typically long-lasting. Common examples of NCDs include cardiovascular diseases, diabetes, cancer, and chronic respiratory diseases etc.

NCDs are chronic in nature and cannot be communicated from one person to another. They are a result of a combination of factors including genetics, physiology, environment and behaviours.

NCDs are caused, to a massive extent, by four behavioural risk factors: tobacco use, unhealthy diet, insufficient physical activity and harmful use of alcohol.

Causes: The causes of NCDs can be divided into three broad categories:

a. modifiable behavioural risk factors,
b. non-modifiable risk factors and
c. metabolic risk factors.

Modifiable behavioural risk factors: Behavioural risk factors such as excessive use of alcohol, bad food habits, eating and smoking tobacco, physical inactivity, wrong body posture and disturbed biological clock increase the likelihood of NCDs. The modern occupational setting (desk jobs) and the stress related to work is also being seen as a potent risk factor for NCDs.

Non-modifiable risk factors: Risk factors that cannot be controlled or modified by the application of an intervention can be called non-modifiable risk factors and include:

- Age, Race, Gender and Genetics

Metabolic risk factors: Metabolic risk factors lead to four major changes in the metabolic systems that increase the possibility of NCDs:

i. Increased blood pressure
ii. Obesity
iii. Increased blood glucose levels or hyperglycaemia
iv. Increased levels of fat in the blood or hyperlipidaemia

CONTROL AND PREVENTION OF NCD'S

An important way of controlling non-communicable diseases is by controlling risk factors associated with it. A number of non-communicable diseases can be prevented by controlling the behavioural or lifestyle habits associated with those diseases.

The 12 (Gift of Modern Life) Lifestyle Disorders of NCD's, we should take seriously:

The shift in purchasing power and the coming in of technology has changed the way our life functions now. Less physical activity, more availability of resources and no time to spare, we have become easy preys to these Lifestyle disorders.

1. **Alzheimers:** A progressive disease that destroys memory and other important mental functions.

   Brain cell connections and the cells themselves degenerate and die, eventually destroying memory and other important mental functions. Memory loss and confusion are the main symptoms. No cure exists, but medication and management strategies may temporarily improve symptoms.

2. **High blood pressure:** Approx. more than100 million people in India suffer from high blood pressure. Some very common reasons for high blood pressure are stress, obesity, genetic factors and unhealthy eating habits. When the reading in the blood pressure machine measures 140/90 or higher, our blood pressure is high. Once this happens, we will feel severe discomfort.

3. **Type II diabetes:** As mentioned in the first point, obesity is one of the primary causes of Type II diabetes. Type II diabetes is the non-insulin form which develops in adults due to poor eating habits and bad lifestyle choices. India has the largest number of diabetics with type II.

4. **Heart diseases:** Any irregularity or abnormality which affects the heart muscle and blood vessel walls can be referred to as a heart disease. Smoking, diabetes and high cholesterol contribute to its development in the body.

    a. **Arteriosclerosis:** Arteriosclerosis occurs when the arterial blood vessel walls thicken and lose elasticity. This usually causes blood circulation disorders, chest pain, and heart attacks. Arteriosclerosis is also linked to obesity, diabetes and high blood pressure. At least 30-40% of cardiovascular deaths happen in the age group of 34-64 in India.

    b. **Stroke:** When the blood vessel carrying blood to the brain has a blockage leading to an oxygen deficiency for the area of the brain it carried blood to, the result of this is called Stroke. High blood pressure, if not taken care of in time, with proper treatment, can lead to a stroke. Stroke can also be caused due to hereditary reasons.

5. **Obesity:** Unhealthy eating habits, stressful lifestyle, reduced physical activity translates to obesity. Anybody who is overweight suffers from breathing

issues, blood pressure, cardiovascular diseases, diabetes etc. This is also the first step to our body attracting all kinds of other lifestyle disorders.

6. **Cancer:** Due to the stressful lifestyle that we lead now, our body's immunity has decreased. This means that the white blood cells lose their power to fight the viruses that enter our body. Because of this, there may be an irregular cell growth, which can be concluded as cancer, if neglected. Cancer can be caused due to many reasons like prolonged smoking (lung cancer), too much exposure to the sun (skin cancer) etc.

7. **Thyroid:** Thyroid disease is a general term for a medical condition for an imbalanced and abnormal functioning of thyroid from making the right amount of hormones. Our thyroid typically makes hormones that keep our body functioning normally. When the thyroid makes too much thyroid hormone, our body uses energy too quickly. This is called **hyperthyroidism**. Using energy too quickly will make us tired — it can make our heart beat faster; it may be a reason to lose weight without trying and even make us feel nervous. On the flip-side of this, our thyroid can make too little thyroid hormone. This is called **hypothyroidism**. When we have too little thyroid hormone in our body, it can make us feel tired, we might gain weight and we may even be unable to tolerate cold temperatures. These two main disorders can be caused by a variety of

conditions. They can also be passed down through families (inherited).

8. **Swimmer's ear:** When we use headphones constantly and are exposed to loud music more than what we should be, the ultimate result of this is swimmer's ear. Swimmer's ear causes inflammation, irritation or infection in the ear canal or the outer ear.

9. **Cirrhosis:** Cirrhosis can be defined as a group of liver disorders. Liver can be severely affected by heavy alcohol consumption and chronic hepatitis. This has become a common lifestyle disease as many people consume alcohol on a daily basis to deal with stress.

10. **Nephritis:** When there is swelling in the kidneys leading to abnormal function, it is known as nephritis. There are many causes of nephritis, one of them being an allergic reaction to a medication or antibiotic. Other than this, it can also be caused due to bacterial infections, which may enter through street foods not prepared in hygienic conditions.

11. **Chronic obstructive pulmonary disease:** COPB is caused by the permanent obstruction of the airways. The increase in air pollution due to factors like gas leaks and smoking can worsen this condition.

12. **PCOS:** PCOD or PCOS is a condition that affects women's ovaries, the reproductive organs that produce progesterone and oestrogen hormones that help in regulating the menstrual cycle and also produce small amount of hormones inhibin, relaxin, and male hormones called androgens.

Almost 10% of women in the world is suffering from PCOD. In compare to PCOD women with PCOS produce higher-than-normal amounts of male hormones. This hormone imbalance causes them to skip menstrual periods and makes it harder for them to get pregnant.

PCOD (Polycytic Ovarian Disease)	PCOS (Polycystic Ovary Syndrome)
PCOD is a common disorder, 10% of world women population affected by it.	PCOS is a serious medical condition around 0.02% to 2.5% of world women population affected by it.
PCOD is a condition in which ovaries produce many immature or partially mature eggs, this happen due to poor lifestyle, obesity, stress and hormonal imbalance.	PCOS is a metabolic disorder and more severe form of PCOD can lead to anovulation where ovaries stop releasing eggs.
PCOD doesn't affect fertility in women, in this condition woman still can ovulate and become pregnant with little help, following medication can complete pregnancy.	PCOS seriously affects fertility in women. Due to PCOS woman cannot ovulate regularly, making them hard to get pregnant. If become pregnant, there is a risk of miscarriage, premature birth or complications in their pregnancy.
PCOD doesn't have any serious complications.	PCOS have serious complications such as type 2 diabetes, heart disease, high-blood pressure and endometrial cancer in later stage.

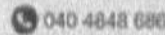

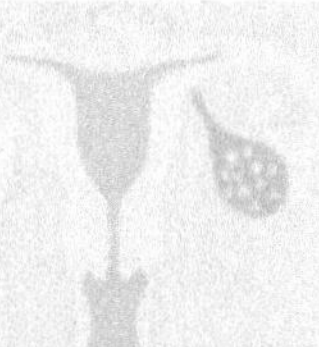

SIGNS AND SYMPTOMS OF
POLYCYSTIC OVARY
SYNDROME (PCOS)

Irregular or
Prolonged
Periods

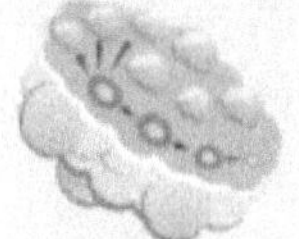

Fluid-Filled
Sacs or
Cysts

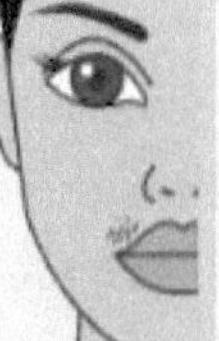

Growth of
Extra,
Unwanted
Hair

Hair
Loss

Excessive
Cramping
& Bloating
During
Menstruation

Acne & Other
Skin Problems

Psychological
Stress &
Depression

Fatigue

Pelvic
Pain

Rapid
Weight
Gain

eMediHealth

THE PRE-REQUISITES FOR NCD's

Pre-requisites for Non-Communicable Diseases (NCDs) refer to the factors or conditions that contribute to the development of these chronic health conditions. NCDs are often the result of complex interactions between genetic, environmental, and lifestyle factors. Here are some key pre-requisites or risk factors for NCDs:

1. **Unhealthy Diet:**
   - Consuming diets high in processed foods, sugary beverages, unhealthy fats, and excessive salt contributes to obesity, diabetes, cardiovascular diseases, and certain cancers.

2. **Lack of Physical Activity:**
   - Sedentary lifestyles with minimal physical activity increase the risk of obesity, diabetes, heart diseases, and other NCDs.

3. **Tobacco Use:**
   - Smoking and tobacco use are major risk factors for heart diseases, stroke, respiratory diseases, and various cancers.

4. **Excessive Alcohol Consumption:**
   - Heavy alcohol consumption is linked to liver diseases, cardiovascular problems, and certain cancers.

5. **Obesity and Overweight:**
   - Being overweight or obese significantly increases the risk of developing diabetes, heart diseases, stroke, and certain cancers.

6. **Genetics and Family History:**
   - Genetic predisposition can play a role in the development of some NCDs. A family history of conditions like diabetes or heart diseases can increase the risk.

7. **Age:**
   - The risk of many NCDs, such as cardiovascular diseases and certain cancers, increases with age.

8. **Socioeconomic Factors:**
   - Low socioeconomic status can lead to limited access to healthcare, unhealthy living conditions, and inadequate nutrition, increasing the risk of NCDs.

9. **Environmental Factors:**
   - Exposure to environmental pollutants, toxins, and unhealthy living conditions can contribute to the development of NCDs.

10. **Stress:**
    - Chronic stress can lead to unhealthy coping behaviours, like overeating or smoking, which increase the risk of NCDs.

11. **Lack of Health Education:**
    - Lack of awareness about healthy lifestyles and NCD risk factors can contribute to unhealthy behaviours.

12. **Access to Healthcare:**
    - Limited access to quality healthcare services and preventive screenings can lead to undiagnosed and untreated NCDs.

13. **Poor Mental Health:**
   - ➢ Conditions like depression and anxiety can contribute to unhealthy lifestyle habits and exacerbate the risk of NCDs.

14. **Hormonal Changes:**
   - ➢ Hormonal changes, such as those occurring during menopause, can increase the risk of certain NCDs like osteoporosis.

15. **Chronic Infections:**
   - ➢ Certain chronic infections, such as Human Papillomavirus (HPV) and Hepatitis B and C, are associated with increased cancer risk.

Preventing NCDs involves addressing these pre-requisites through health education, policy interventions, promoting healthy lifestyles, and ensuring access to quality healthcare. Efforts should focus on reducing risk factors and creating environments that support healthy choices.

THE 'PST' APPROACH TO NCD's

The Prevention, Screening and Treatment Approach to Non-Communicable Diseases.

Prevention, screening, and treatment are crucial aspects in managing NCDs.

Here's a brief overview of the 'PST' approach:

1. **Prevention of NCDs:** Preventing NCDs involves adopting healthy lifestyles and minimizing risk factors. Strategies include:

> **Healthy Diet:** Consuming a balanced diet rich in fruits, vegetables, whole grains, lean proteins, and healthy fats. Reducing salt, sugar, and processed foods is important.

> **Regular Physical Activity:** Engaging in regular exercise, such as brisk walking, jogging, swimming, or yoga, can help to maintain a healthy weight and support overall cardiovascular health.

> **Avoiding Tobacco and Alcohol:** Quitting smoking and limiting alcohol consumption significantly reduce the risk of NCDs.

> **Stress Management:** Stress management techniques like meditation, deep breathing, and mindfulness can help lower stress-related risks.

> **Maintaining a Healthy Weight:** Maintaining a healthy Body Mass Index (BMI) reduces the risk of diabetes, heart disease, and other NCDs.

> **Regular Health Check-ups:** Periodic health check-ups helps to identify risk factors early and allow for timely interventions. (Very Important factor for todays Modern Life)

2. **Screening for NCDs:** Early detection of NCDs can lead to better outcomes. Screening tests include:

> **Blood Pressure Measurement:** Regular monitoring of blood pressure helps to detect

hypertension, a significant risk factor for heart diseases and stroke.

> **Blood Glucose Test:** This test checks for diabetes or prediabetes. Early detection and management can prevent complications.

> **Cholesterol Levels:** High cholesterol levels contribute to heart disease risk. Regular cholesterol checks help manage this risk.

> **Cancer Screenings:** Mammograms, Pap tests, colonoscopies, and other cancer-specific screenings help detect cancers early when treatment is more effective.

> **Lung Function Tests:** For those at risk of chronic respiratory diseases, lung function tests help detect conditions like chronic obstructive pulmonary disease (COPD).

3. **Treatment of NCDs:** Treatment of NCDs involves medical interventions and lifestyle modifications:

> **Medications:** Doctors may prescribe medications to manage conditions like high blood pressure, diabetes, and cholesterol.

> **Surgery:** In some cases, surgical interventions are necessary, such as bypass surgery for heart diseases or surgery to remove cancerous tumors – (a swelling of a part of the body, generally without inflammation, caused by an abnormal growth of tissue)

> **Lifestyle Modifications:** Patients are advised to follow healthy lifestyles, including diet

and exercise changes, stress reduction, and medication adherence.

> **Rehabilitation:** For conditions like heart diseases, cardiac rehabilitation programs help patients to recover and manage their condition.

> **Supportive Care:** Patients with chronic diseases benefit from a multidisciplinary approach, including nutrition counseling, physical therapy, and emotional support.

Prevention, screening, and treatment of NCDs require collaboration between individuals, family supports, healthcare providers, communities, and governments. Public health initiatives, health education, and accessible healthcare services play a vital role in reducing the burden of NCDs and improving overall population health.

THE MOST COMMON LIFESTYLE DISORDERS – (ABCD-OPT)

1. ALZHEIMER'S
2. BLOOD PRESSURE
3. CANCER
4. DIABETES
5. OBESITY
6. PCOS
7. THYROID

1. ALZHEIMER'S

Alzheimer's disease is a neurological condition in which the death of brain cells causes memory loss and cognitive decline. It is the most common type of **Dementia** – (A general term for the loss of memory, language, problem-solving and other thinking abilities that are severe enough to interfere with daily life).

A progressive disease that destroys memory and other important mental functions

Brain cell connections and the cells themselves degenerate and die, eventually destroying memory and other important mental functions. Memory loss and confusion are the main symptoms. No cure exists, but medication and management strategies may temporarily improve symptoms.

Alzheimer's disease is a progressive condition, meaning that the symptoms get worse over time. Memory loss is a key feature, and this tends to be one of the first symptoms to develop.

The symptoms appear gradually, over months or years. If they develop over hours or days, a person may require medical attention, as this could indicate a stroke.

Symptoms of Alzheimer's disease include:

- **Memory loss:** A person may have difficulty taking in new information and remembering information. This can lead to:
    - ➤ repeating questions or conversations
    - ➤ losing objects
    - ➤ forgetting about events or appointments
    - ➤ wandering or getting lost

- **Cognitive deficits:** A person may experience difficulty with reasoning, complex tasks, and judgment. This can lead to:
  - ➤ a reduced understanding of safety and risks
  - ➤ difficulty with money or paying bills
  - ➤ difficulty making decisions
  - ➤ difficulty completing tasks that have several stages, such as getting dressed etc.
- **Problems with recognition:** A person may become less able to recognize faces or objects or less able to use basic tools. These issues are not due to problems with eyesight.
- **Problems with spatial awareness:** A person may have difficulty with their balance, trip over, or spill things more often, or they may have difficulty orienting clothing to their body when getting dressed.
- **Problems with speaking, reading, or writing:** A person may develop difficulties with thinking of common words, or they may make more speech, spelling, or writing errors.
- **Personality or behaviour changes:** A person may experience changes in personality and behaviour that include:
  - ➤ becoming upset, angry, or worried more often than before
  - ➤ a loss of interest in or motivation for activities they usually enjoy
  - ➤ a loss of empathy
  - ➤ compulsive, obsessive, or socially inappropriate behaviour

STEP-BY-STEP GUIDE: PROGRESSION OF ALZHEIMER'S DISEASES

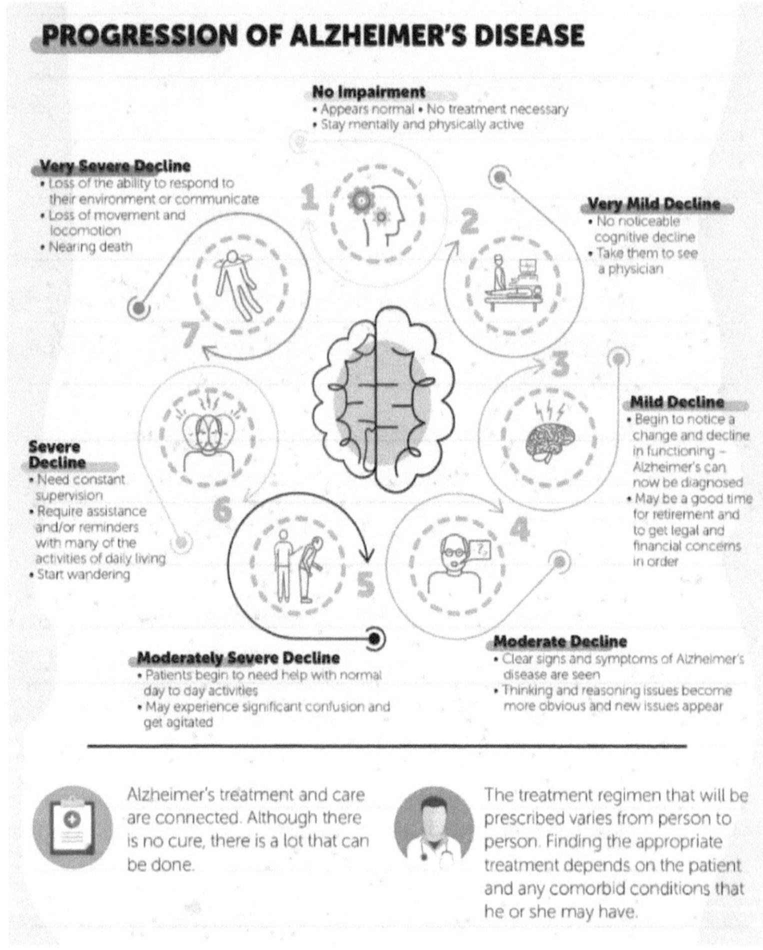

Alzheimer's treatment and care are connected. Although there is no cure, there is a lot that can be done.

The treatment regimen that will be prescribed varies from person to person. Finding the appropriate treatment depends on the patient and any comorbid conditions that he or she may have.

 # Changes in the brain in the Alzheimer's Disease

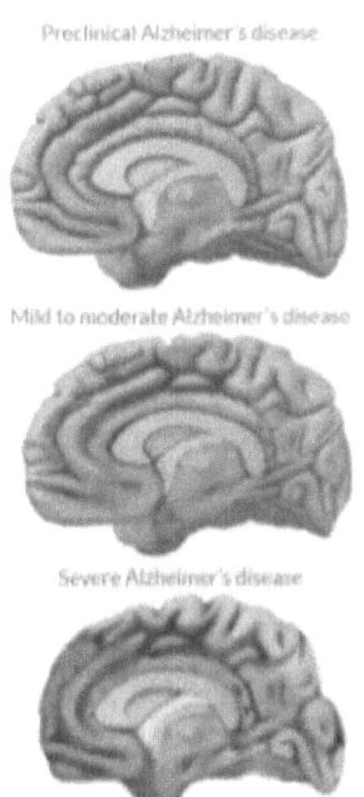

Neurons lose their ability to function and communicate with each other, and eventually they die.

Basically Alzheimer's Disease have 3 stages which are the Very early Alzheimer's, Mild to Moderate Alzheimer's and Severe Alzheimer's.

As Alzheimer's disease progresses, neurofibrillary tangles spread throughout the brain. Plaques also spread throughout the brain, starting in the neocortex. By the final stage, damage is widespread, and brain tissue has shrunk significantly.

STAGES OF ALZHEIMER'S

Alzheimer's disease typically progresses slowly in three general stages: early, middle and late (sometimes referred to as mild, moderate and severe in a medical context). Since Alzheimer's affects people in different ways, each person may experience symptoms — or progress through the stages — differently.

OVERVIEW OF DISEASE PROGRESSION

The symptoms of Alzheimer's disease worsen over time, although the rate at which the disease progresses vary. On average, a person with Alzheimer's lives four to eight years after diagnosis, but can live as long as 20 years, depending on other factors. Changes in the brain related to Alzheimer's begin years before any signs of the disease. This time period, which can last for years, is referred to as preclinical Alzheimer's disease.

The stages below provide an overall idea of how abilities change once symptoms appear and should only be used as a general guide.

The stages are separated into three categories: mild Alzheimer's disease, moderate Alzheimer's disease and severe Alzheimer's disease. Be aware that it may be difficult to place a person with Alzheimer's in a specific stage as stages may overlap.

EARLY-STAGE ALZHEIMER'S (MILD)

In the early stage of Alzheimer's, a person may function independently. He or she may still drive, work and be part of social activities. Despite this, the person may feel as if he or she is having memory lapses, such as forgetting familiar words or the location of everyday objects.

Symptoms may not be widely apparent at this stage, but family and close friends may take notice and a doctor would be able to identify symptoms using certain diagnostic tools.

Common difficulties include:

- Coming up with the right word or name.
- Remembering names when introduced to new people.
- Having difficulty performing tasks in social or work settings.
- Forgetting material that was just read.
- Losing or misplacing a valuable object.
- Experiencing increased trouble with planning or organizing.

MIDDLE-STAGE ALZHEIMER'S (MODERATE)

Middle-stage Alzheimer's is typically the longest stage and can last for many years. As the disease progresses, the person with Alzheimer's will require a greater level of care. During the middle stage of Alzheimer's, the dementia symptoms are more pronounced, the person may confuse words, get frustrated or angry, and act in an unexpected ways, such as refusing to bathe etc. Damage to nerve cells in the brain can also make it difficult for the person to express thoughts and perform routine tasks without assistance.

Symptoms, which vary from person to person, may include:

- Being forgetful of events or personal history.
- Feeling moody or withdrawn, especially in socially or mentally challenging situations.
- Being unable to recall information about themselves like their address or telephone number, and the high school or college they attended.
- Experiencing confusion about where they are or what day it is.
- Requiring help choosing proper clothing for the season or the occasion.
- Having trouble controlling their bladder and bowels.
- Experiencing changes in sleep patterns – sleeping during the day & becoming restless at night.
- Showing an increased tendency to wander and become lost.
- Demonstrating personality and behavioural changes, including suspiciousness and delusions

or compulsive, repetitive behaviour like hand-wringing or tissue shredding.

In the middle stage, the person living with Alzheimer's can still participate in daily activities with assistance. It's important to find out what the person can still do or find ways to simplify tasks. As the need for more intensive care increases, caregivers may want to consider respite care or an adult day-care centre, so they can have a temporary break from caregiving, while the person living with Alzheimer's continues to receive care in a safe environment.

LATE-STAGE ALZHEIMER'S (SEVERE)

In the final stage of the disease, dementia symptoms are severe. Individuals lose the ability to respond to their environment, to carry on a conversation and, eventually, to control movement. They may still say words or phrases, but communicating pain becomes difficult. As memory and cognitive skills continue to worsen, significant personality changes may take place and individuals need extensive care

At this stage, individuals may:

- Require around-the-clock assistance with daily personal care.
- Lose awareness of recent experiences as well as of their surroundings.
- Experience changes in physical abilities, including walking, sitting and, eventually, swallowing
- Have difficulty communicating.
- Become vulnerable to infections, especially pneumonia.

The person living with Alzheimer's may not be able to initiate engagement as much during the late stage, but he or she can still benefit from interaction in ways that are appropriate, like listening to relaxing music or receiving reassurance through gentle touch. During this stage, caregivers may want to use support services, such as hospice care, which focus on providing comfort and dignity at the end of life. Hospice can be of great benefit to people in the final stages of Alzheimer's and other dementias and their families.

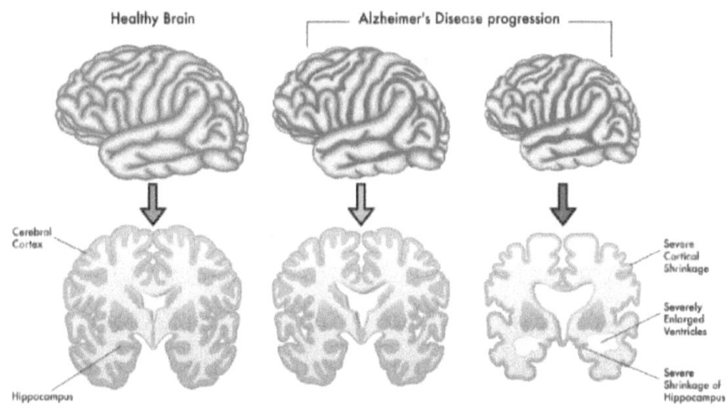

The Diminishing Views of Brain in Alzhemiers

2. BLOOD PRESSURE

Blood pressure is the force that a person's blood exerts against the walls of their blood vessels. This pressure depends on the resistance of the blood vessels and how hard the heart has to work.

HYPERTENSION (HIGH BLOOD PRESSURE) is another name for high blood pressure. It can lead to severe health complications and increase the risk of heart disease, stroke, and sometimes death.

High blood pressure (hypertension) is a common condition in which the long-term force of the blood against our artery walls is high enough that it may eventually cause health problems, such as heart disease.

HYPOTENSION (LOW BLOOD PRESSURE) is the medical term for low blood pressure (less than 90/60).

Optimal blood pressure is less than 120/80 (systolic/diastolic). In healthy people, low blood pressure without any symptoms is not usually a concern and does not need to be treated. But low blood pressure can be a sign of an underlying problem – especially in the elderly – where it may cause inadequate blood flow to the heart, brain, and other vital organs.

BLOOD PRESSURE is determined both by the amount of blood our heart pumps and the amount of resistance to blood flow in our arteries. The more blood our heart pumps and the narrower your arteries, the higher our blood pressure. A blood pressure reading is given in millimeters of mercury (mm Hg). It has two numbers.

- Top number **(systolic pressure).** The first, or upper, number **measures the pressure** in our arteries **when our heart beats**.
- Bottom number **(diastolic pressure).** The second, or lower, number **measures the pressure** in our arteries **between beats**.

DIFFERENT STAGES OF BLOOD PRESSURE & RECOMMENDED PRECAUTIONARY MEASURES

Stage	Systolic BP (mmHg)		Diastolic BP (mmHg)	Action
Normal and optimal	Below 130	and	Below 85	Keep up the good work and stick with heart-healthy habits
High normal	130 - 139	or	85 – 89	Make lifestyle changes to lower blood pressure
Mild hypertension	140 – 159	or	90 – 99	See a doctor or GP as soon as possible
Moderate hypertension	160 – 179	or	100 – 109	See a doctor or GP as soon as possible
Hypertensive emergency	above 180	or	above 110	Requires emergency medical attention. Go to a hospital

PRECAUTIONARY NOTE: It's important to consult with a qualified healthcare professional to interpret these results accurately. They will consider the individual's symptoms, medical history, and overall health to make an informed diagnosis and recommendations.

EFFECTS OF HIGH BLOOD PRESSURE ON THE BODY

Because hypertension is often a silent condition, it can cause damage to our body for years before symptoms become obvious. If hypertension isn't treated, we may face serious, even fatal, complications.

Complications of hypertension include the following.

I) DAMAGED ARTERIES

Healthy arteries are flexible and strong. Blood flows freely and unobstructed through healthy arteries and vessels.

Hypertension makes arteries tougher, tighter, and less elastic. This damage makes it easier for dietary fats to deposit in our arteries and restrict blood flow. This damage can lead to increased blood pressure, blockages, and, eventually, heart attack and stroke.

II) DAMAGED HEART

Hypertension makes our heart work too hard. The increased pressure in your blood vessels forces your heart's muscles to pump more frequently and with more force than a healthy heart should have to.

This may cause an enlarged heart. An enlarged heart increases our risk for the following:

- heart failure
- arrhythmias
- sudden cardiac death
- heart attack

ATHEROS-CLE-ROSIS: Is a specific type of Arteriosclerosis. It is the build-up of fats, cholesterol & other substances in & on the artery walls. This build-up is called plaque. The plaque can cause the arteries to narrow, blocking blood flow. It can also burst, leading to a blood clot.

Although Atherosclerosis is often considered a heart problem, it can affect arteries anywhere in the body.

It can be treated as Healthy Lifestyle Habits can help to prevent it.

CHOLESTROL LEVEL GUIDELINESS

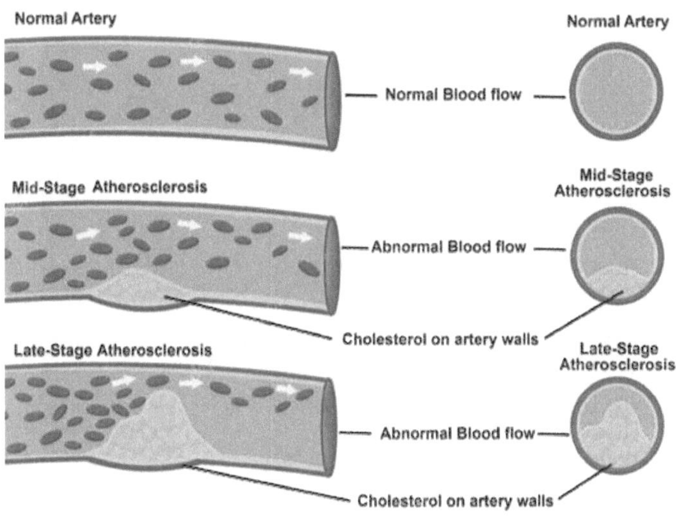

National Cholesterol Education Program Cholesterol Guidelines			
	Desirable	Borderline High	High
Total Cholesterol	Less than 200	200 - 239	240 and higher
LDL Cholesterol (the "bad" cholesterol)	Less than 130	130 - 159	160 and higher
HDL Cholesterol (the "good" cholesterol)	50 and higher	40 - 49	Less than 40
Triglycerides	Less than 200	200 - 399	400 and higher

PRECAUTIONARY NOTE: It's important to consult with a qualified healthcare professional to interpret these results accurately. They will consider the individual's symptoms, medical history, and overall health to make an informed diagnosis and recommendations.

III) DAMAGED BRAIN

Our brain relies on a healthy supply of oxygen-rich blood to work properly. High blood pressure can reduce our brain's supply of blood:

- Temporary blockages of blood flow to the brain are called transient ischemic attacks (TIAs).
- Significant blockages of blood flow cause brain cells to die. This is known as a Stroke.

Uncontrolled hypertension may also affect our memory and ability to learn, recall, speak, and reason. Treating hypertension often doesn't erase or reverse the effects of uncontrolled hypertension. It does, however, lower the risks for future problems.

DIETARY RECOMMENDATIONS FOR PEOPLE WITH HIGH BLOOD PRESSURE

One of the easiest ways we can treat hypertension and prevent possible complications is through our diet. What we eat can go a long way toward easing or eliminating hypertension.

Here are some of the most common dietary recommendations for people with hypertension.

EAT LESS MEAT, MORE PLANTS

A plant-based diet is an easy way to increase fibre and reduce the amount of sodium and unhealthy saturated and trans-fat, we take in from dairy foods and meat. Increase the number of fruits, vegetables, leafy greens, and whole grains eating. Instead of red meat, opt for healthier lean proteins like fish, poultry, or tofu.

REDUCE DIETARY SODIUM

People with hypertension and those with an increased risk for heart disease may need to keep their daily sodium intake between 1,500 milligrams and 2,300 milligrams per day. The best way to reduce sodium is to cook fresh foods more often. Avoid eating restaurant food or prepackaged foods, which are often very high in sodium.

CUT BACK ON SWEETS

Sugary foods and beverages contain empty calories but don't have nutritional content. If you want something sweet, try eating fresh fruit or small amounts of dark chocolate that haven't been sweetened as much with sugar. Studies trusted source suggest regularly eating dark chocolate may reduce blood pressure.

MONITOR YOUR BLOOD PRESSURE REGULARLY

The best way to prevent complications and avoid problems is to catch hypertension early. You can come into your doctor's clinic for a blood pressure reading, or the doctor may ask to purchase a blood pressure machine and take readings at home.

Keep a log of our blood pressure readings and take it to your regular doctor appointments. This can help your doctor to checkmany possible problems before the condition advances.

Did you know ... Maintaining a healthy diet low in fat, sugar and salt can help bring your blood pressure to a healthier range?

AGE	Average	Minimum	Maximum
14–19	117/77	105/73	120/81
20–24	120/79	108/75	132/83
25–29	121/80	109/76	133/84
30–34	122/81	110/77	134/85
35–39	123/82	111/78	135/86
40–44	125/83	112/79	137/87
45–49	127/84	115/80	139/88
50–54	129/85	116/81	142/89
55–59	131/86	118/82	144/90

Women's Blood Pressure Limits by Age

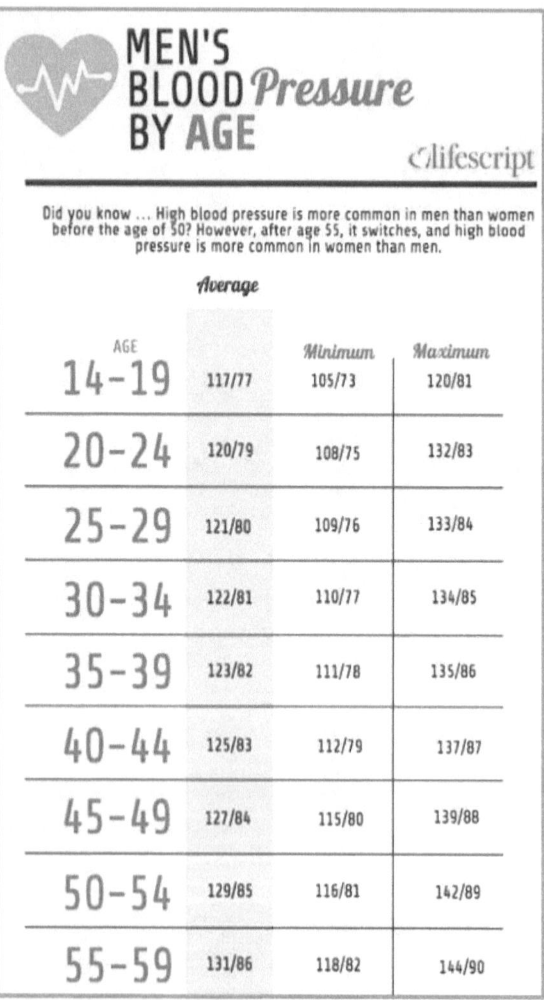

AGE	Average	Minimum	Maximum
14–19	117/77	105/73	120/81
20–24	120/79	108/75	132/83
25–29	121/80	109/76	133/84
30–34	122/81	110/77	134/85
35–39	123/82	111/78	135/86
40–44	125/83	112/79	137/87
45–49	127/84	115/80	139/88
50–54	129/85	116/81	142/89
55–59	131/86	118/82	144/90

Men's Blood Pressure Limits by Age

PRECAUTIONARY NOTE: It's important to consult with a qualified healthcare professional to interpret these results accurately. They will consider the individual's symptoms, medical history, and overall health to make an informed diagnosis and recommendations.

3. CANCER

I) CANCER FACTS

- Cancer is the uncontrolled growth of abnormal cells anywhere in a body.

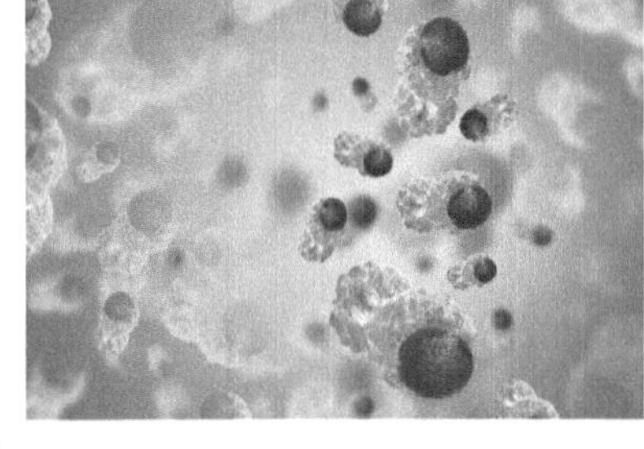

- There are over 200 types of cancer.

- Anything that may cause a normal body cell to develop abnormally and potentially, can cause cancer; general categories of cancer-related or causative agents are as follows: chemical or toxic compound exposures, ionizing radiation, some pathogens, and human genetics.

- Cancer symptoms and signs depend on the specific type and grade of cancer; although general signs and symptoms are not very specific, the following can be found in patients with different cancers: fatigue, weight loss, pain, skin changes, change in bowel or bladder function, unusual bleeding, persistent cough or voice change, fever, lumps, or tissue masses.

- Although there are many tests to screen and presumptively diagnose cancer, the definite diagnosis is made by examination of a **Biopsy** sample of suspected cancer tissue.

- Cancer staging is often determined by biopsy results and helps to determine the cancer type and the extent of cancer spread; Staging also helps caregivers determine treatment protocols. In general, in most staging methods, the higher the number assigned (usually between 0 to 4), the more aggressive the cancer type or the more widespread is cancer in the body. Staging methods differ from cancer to cancer and need to be individually discussed with our health care provider.

- Treatment protocols vary according to the type and stage of cancer. Most treatment protocols are designed to fit the individual patient's disease. However, most treatments include at least one of the following and may include all: surgery, chemotherapy, and radiation therapy.

- There are many listed home remedies and alternative treatments for cancers but patients are strongly recommended to discuss these before use with their cancer doctors.

- The prognosis of cancer can range from excellent to poor. The prognosis depends on the cancer type and its staging with those cancers known to be aggressive and those staged with higher numbers (3 to 4) often have a prognosis that ranges more towards poor.

II) KEY RISK FACTOR OF CANCER

Many things can cause cell abnormalities and have been linked to cancer development. Some cancer causes remain unknown while other cancers have environmental or lifestyle triggers or may develop from more than one known cause.

Some may be developmentally influenced by a person's genetic makeup. Many patients develop cancer due to a combination of these factors; it is often difficult or impossible to determine the initiating event(s) that cause cancer to develop in a specific person, research has provided clinicians with a number of likely causes that alone or in concert with other causes, are the likely candidates for initiating cancer.

- **Factors That are Known to Increase the Risk of Cancer**
  - Cigarette Smoking and Tobacco Use
  - Infections
  - Radiation
  - Immunosuppressive Medicines After Organ Transplant
- **Factors That May Affect the Risk of Cancer**
  - Diet
  - Alcohol
  - Physical Activity
  - Obesity
  - Diabetes
  - Environmental Risk Factor
- **The three most common cancers in men, women, and children are as follows:**
  - **Men**: Prostate, lung, and colorectal
  - **Women**: Breast, lung, and colorectal
  - **Children**: Leukemia, brain tumors, and lymphoma

III) CANCER SYMPTOMS & SIGNS

The American Cancer Society describes seven warning signs and/or symptoms that cancer may be present, and which should prompt a person to seek medical attention. The word "**CAUTION**" can help us to remember these.

- **C**hange in bowel or bladder habits
- **A** sore throat that does not heal
- **U**nusual bleeding or discharge (e.g. nipple secretions or a "sore" that will not heal that oozes material)
- **T**hickening or lump in the breast, testicles, or elsewhere
- **I**ndigestion (usually chronic) or difficulty in swallowing
- **O**bvious change in the size, color, shape, or thickness of a wart or mole
- **N**agging cough or hoarseness

Other signs or symptoms may also alert us or our doctor to the possibility of having some form of cancer. These include the following:

- Unexplained loss of weight or loss of appetite
- A new type of pain in the bones or other parts of the body that may be steadily worsening, or come and go, but is unlike previous pains one has had before.
- Persistent fatigue, nausea, or vomiting
- Unexplained low-grade fevers may be either persistent or come and go
- Recurring infections which will not clear with usual treatment

Anyone, with these signs and symptoms should consult their doctor; these symptoms may also arise from non-cancerous conditions.

IV) CAUSES OF CANCER

Certain genes control the life cycle—the growth, function, division, and death – of a cell. When these genes are damaged, the balance between normal cell growth and death is lost. Cancer cells are caused by DNA damage and out-of-control cell growth. The following is a partial list of factors known to damage DNA and increase the risk of cancer

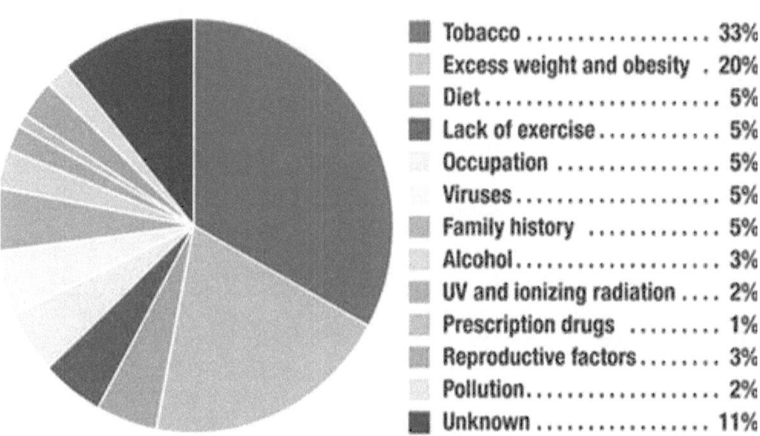

Cancer refers to any one of a large number of diseases characterized by the development of abnormal cells that divide uncontrollably and have the ability to infiltrate and destroy normal body tissue. Cancer often has the ability to spread throughout our body.

Cancer is the second-leading cause of death in the world. But survival rates are improving for many types of cancer, thanks to improvements in cancer screening, treatment and prevention.

V) STAGES OF CANCER

Stages of Cancer
Marshfield Clinic

Stage 1 — Early Stage
- A small, invasive mass or tumor has been found.
- No spread to lymph nodes or other tissues.
- Sometimes called early-stage or "localized" cancer.

Stage 2 — Localized
- Cancer has started to affect nearby tissue.
- Mass may have grown in size.
- Spread to lymph nodes near the mass.

Stage 3 — Regional Spread
- Cancer affects more surrounding tissue.
- Mass may have grown in size.
- Spread to distant lymph nodes away from the mass.

Stage 4 — Distant Spread
- Cancer has spread to other tissues or organs beyond the region where it originated.
- Sometimes called advanced or "metastatic" cancer.

For more cancer topics and advice visit:
www.shine365.marshfieldclinic.org/category/cancer-care

To learn about oncology specialty services at Marshfield Clinic:
www.marshfieldclinic.org/specialties/cancer-care

Shine 365
Marshfield Clinic

Stages of Cancer Development

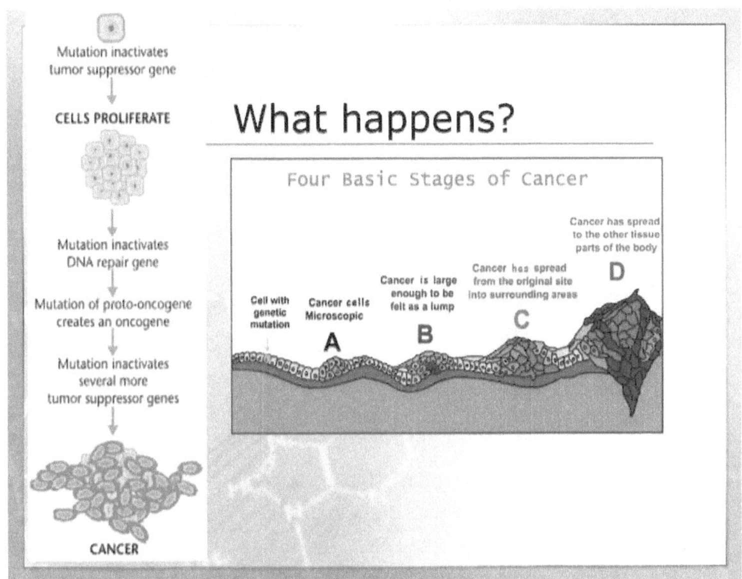

Cancer Cell Development Image in 4 Different Stages

VI) PREVENTION OF CANCER

WAYS TO REDUCE THE RISK OF CANCER

Doctors have identified several ways to reduce risk of cancer, such as:

- **Stop smoking:** If we smoke, **QUIT**. If we don't smoke, don't start. Smoking is linked to several types of cancer – not just lung cancer. Stopping now will reduce our risk of cancer in the future.

- **Avoid excessive sun exposure:** Harmful ultraviolet (UV) rays from the sun can increase our risk of skin cancer. Limit the sun exposure by staying in the shade, wearing protective clothing or applying sunscreen.

- **Eat a healthy diet:** Choose a diet rich in fruits and vegetables. Select whole grains and lean proteins. Limit intake of processed foods & meats.
- **Exercise most days of the week:** Regular exercise is linked to a lower risk of cancer. Aim for at least 30 minutes of exercise most days of the week. If we haven't been exercising regularly, start out slowly and work way up to 30 minutes or longer.
- **Maintain a healthy weight:** Being overweight or obese may increase risk of cancer. Work to achieve and maintain a healthy weight through a combination of a healthy diet and regular exercise.
- **Drink alcohol in moderation:** If we choose to drink alcohol, do so in moderation. For healthy adults, that means – up to **one** drink a day for **women** and up to **two** drinks a day for men.
- **Schedule cancer screening tests:** Talk to doctor about what types of cancer screening tests are best suited for you based on your risk factors.
- **Ask your doctor about immunizations:** Certain viruses increase our risk of cancer. Immunizations may help prevent those viruses, including hepatitis B, which increases the risk of liver cancer, and human papillomavirus (HPV), which increases the risk of cervical cancer and other cancers. Ask your doctor whether immunization against these viruses is appropriate for you.

4. DIABETES

DIABETES MANAGEMENT & GUIDE:

Diabetes mellitus refers to a group of diseases that affect how our body uses blood sugar (glucose). Glucose is vital to our health because it's an important source of energy for the cells that make up our muscles and tissues. It's also our brain's main source of fuel.

The underlying cause of diabetes varies by type. But, no matter what type of diabetes we have, it can lead to excess sugar in our blood. Too much sugar in our blood can lead to serious health problems.

SYMPTOMS

Diabetes symptoms vary depending on how much our blood sugar is elevated. Some people, especially those with prediabetes or type 2 diabetes, may not experience symptoms initially. In type 1 diabetes, symptoms tend to come on quickly and be more severe.

Some of the signs and symptoms of type 1 and type 2 diabetes are:

- Increased thirst
- Frequent urination
- Extreme hunger
- Unexplained weight loss
- Presence of ketones in the urine (ketones are a byproduct of the breakdown of muscle and fat that happens when there's not enough available insulin)

- Fatigue
- Irritability
- Blurred vision
- Slow-healing sores
- Frequent infections, such as gums or skin infections and vaginal infections

Type 1 diabetes can develop at any age, though it often appears during childhood or adolescence.

Type 2 diabetes, the more common type, can develop at any age, though it's more common in people older than 40+ years.

PREVENTION

Type 1 diabetes can't be prevented. However, the same healthy lifestyle choices that help to treat prediabetes, or type 2 diabetes and gestational diabetes can also help to prevent them:

- **Eat healthy foods:** Choose foods lower in fat and calories and higher in fibre. Focus on fruits, vegetables and whole grains. Strive for variety to prevent boredom.
- **Get more physical activity:** Aim for 30 minutes of moderate physical activity a day. Take a brisk daily walk, after getting up from bed in morning and post dinner in night. Ride your bike. Swim laps. If you can't fit in a long workout, break it up into smaller sessions spread throughout the day.

- **Lose excess pounds:** If you're overweight, losing even 7 percent of your body weight can reduce the risk of diabetes.

Don't try to lose weight during pregnancy, however. Talk to your doctor about how much weight is healthy for you to gain during pregnancy.

To keep your weight in a healthy range, focus on permanent changes to your eating and exercise habits. Motivate yourself by remembering the benefits of losing weight, such as a healthier heart, more energy and improved self-esteem.

COMPLICATIONS

Long-term complications of diabetes develop gradually. The longer you have diabetes – and the less controlled your blood sugar – the higher the risk of complications. Eventually, diabetes complications may be disabling or even life-threatening. Possible complications include:

- **Cardiovascular disease:** Diabetes dramatically increases the risk of various cardiovascular problems, including coronary artery disease with chest pain (angina), heart attack, stroke and narrowing of arteries (atherosclerosis). If you have diabetes, you're more likely to have heart disease or stroke.
- **Nerve damage:** Excess sugar can injure the walls of the tiny blood vessels (capillaries) that nourish your nerves, especially in your legs. This can cause tingling, numbness, burning or pain that usually

begins at the tips of the toes or fingers and gradually spreads upward.

Left untreated, you could lose all sense of feeling in the affected limbs. Damage to the nerves related to digestion can cause problems with nausea, vomiting, diarrhoea or constipation. For men, it may lead to erectile dysfunction.

- **Kidney damage:** The kidneys contain millions of tiny blood vessel clusters (glomeruli) that filter waste from your blood. Diabetes can damage this delicate filtering system. Severe damage can lead to kidney failure or irreversible end-stage kidney disease, which may require dialysis or a kidney transplant.

- **Eye damage:** Diabetes can damage the blood vessels of the retina (diabetic retinopathy), potentially leading to blindness. Diabetes also increases the risk of other serious vision conditions, such as cataracts and glaucoma.

- **Foot damage:** Nerve damage in the feet or poor blood flow to the feet increases the risk of various foot complications. Left untreated, cuts and blisters can develop serious infections, which often heal poorly. These infections may ultimately require toe, foot or leg amputation.

- **Skin conditions:** Diabetes may leave you more susceptible to skin problems, including bacterial and fungal infections.

- **Hearing impairment:** Hearing problems are more common in people with diabetes.
- **Alzheimer's disease:** Type 2 diabetes may increase the risk of dementia, such as Alzheimer's disease. The poorer your blood sugar control, the greater the risk appears to be. Although there are theories as to how these disorders might be connected, none has yet been proved.
- **Depression:** Depression symptoms are common in people with type 1 and type 2 diabetes. Depression can affect diabetes management.

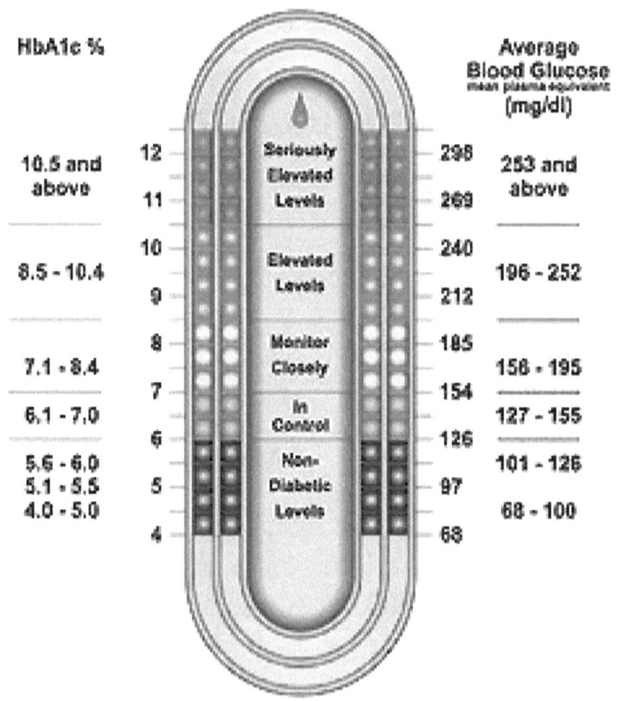

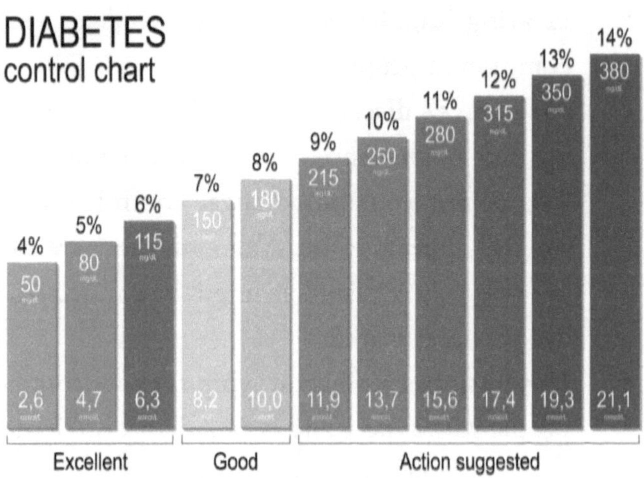

Blood Sugar Levels – Normal & Diagnostic Ranges

A GUIDE TO BLOOD SUGAR LEVELS

BLOOD SUGAR LEVEL CHART			
	FASTING	**JUST ATE**	**3 HOURS AFTER EATING**
NORMAL	80-100	170-200	120-140
PRE-DIABETIC	101-125	190-230	140-160
DIABETIC	126+	220-300	200+

PRECAUTIONARY NOTE: It's important to consult with a qualified healthcare professional to interpret these results accurately. They will consider the individual's symptoms, medical history, and overall health to make an informed diagnosis and recommendations.

5. OBESITY

OBESITY FACTS

Body mass index (BMI) is a calculation that takes a person's weight and height into account to measure body size. [BMI = W/HxH] = Weight in KG / Height x Height in Meter.

In adults, obesity is defined as having a BMI of 30.0 or more – according to the Centre for Disease Control and Prevention (CDC).

Obesity is associated with a higher risk for serious diseases, such as type 2 diabetes, heart disease, and cancer.

According to the CDC Trusted Source: "Factors such as age, sex, ethnicity, and muscle mass can influence the relationship between BMI and body fat. Also, BMI doesn't distinguish between excess fat, muscle, or bone mass, nor does it provide any indication of the distribution of fat among individuals."

Despite these limitations, BMI continues to be widely used as a way to measure body size.

OBESITY CLASSIFICATION

The following classes Trusted Source are used for adults – above 20 years old.

BMI	Class
18.5 or under	underweight
18.5 to <25.0	"normal" weight
25.0 to <30.0	overweight
30.0 to <35.0	class 1 obesity
35.0 to <40.0	class 2 obesity
40.0 or over	class 3 obesity (also known as morbid, extreme, or severe obesity)

PRECAUTIONARY NOTE: It's important to consult with a qualified healthcare professional to interpret these results accurately. They will consider the individual's symptoms, medical history, and overall health to make an informed diagnosis and recommendations.

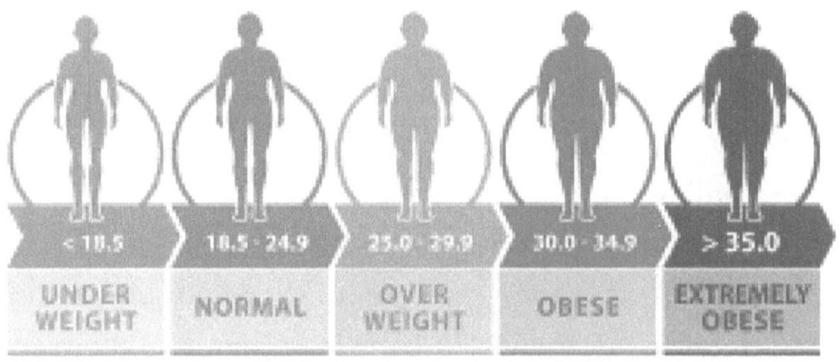

Pictorial Representation of BMI

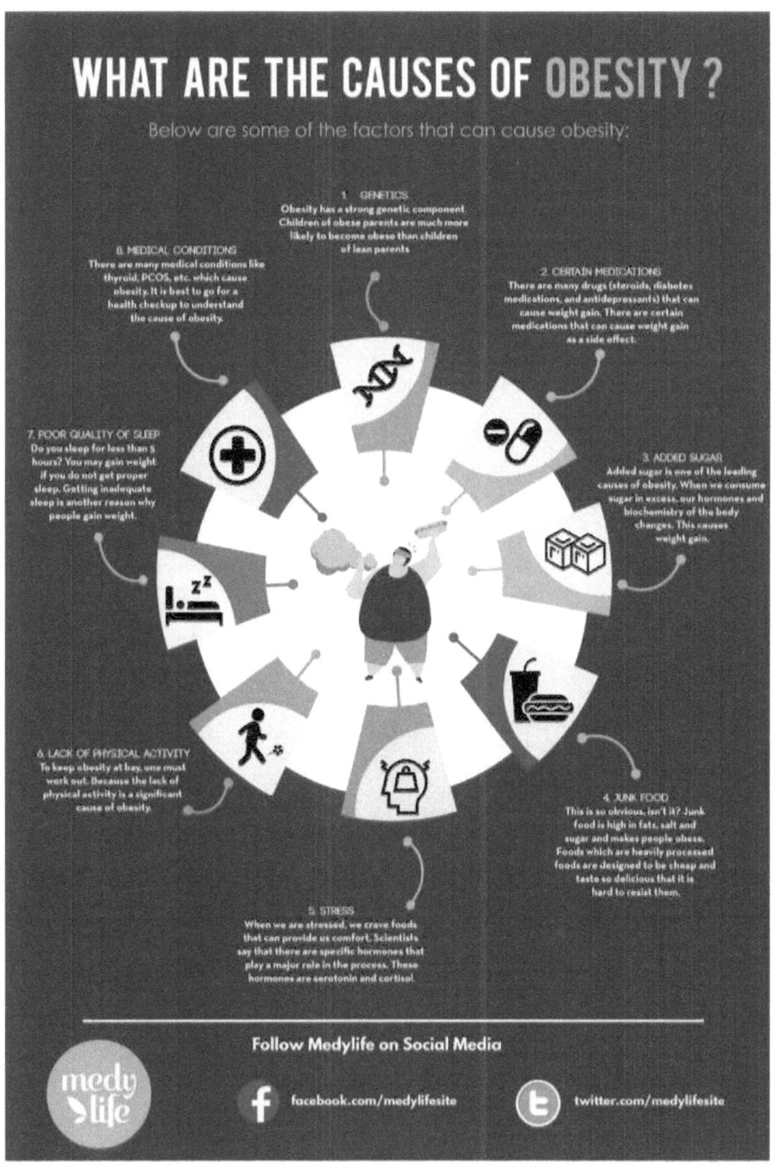

Causes of Obesity

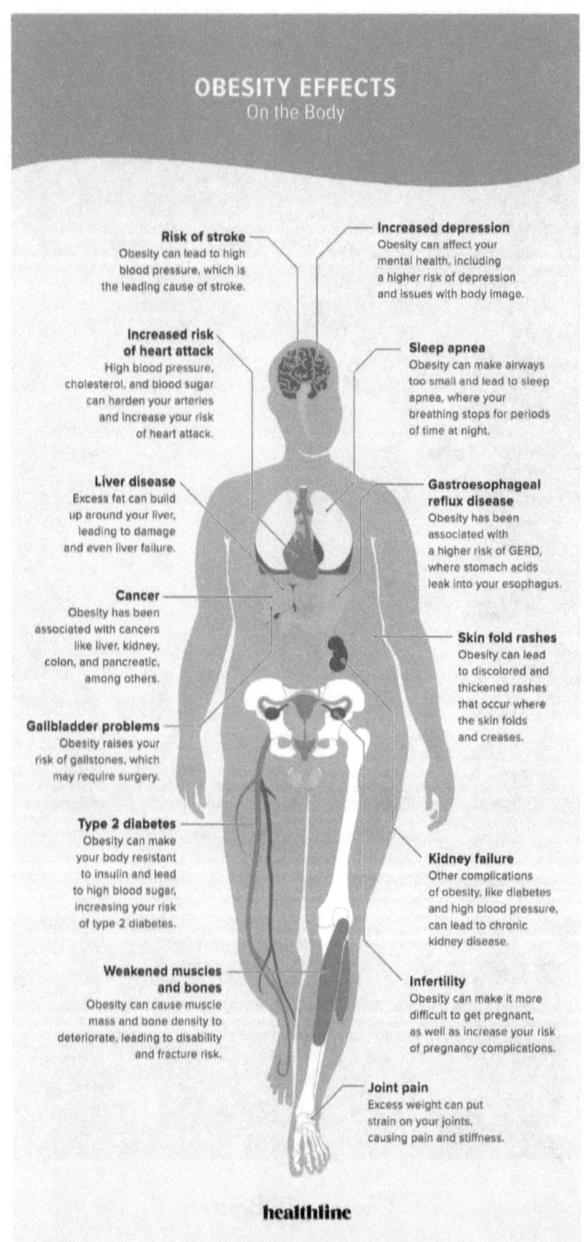

Obesity Effects on the Body

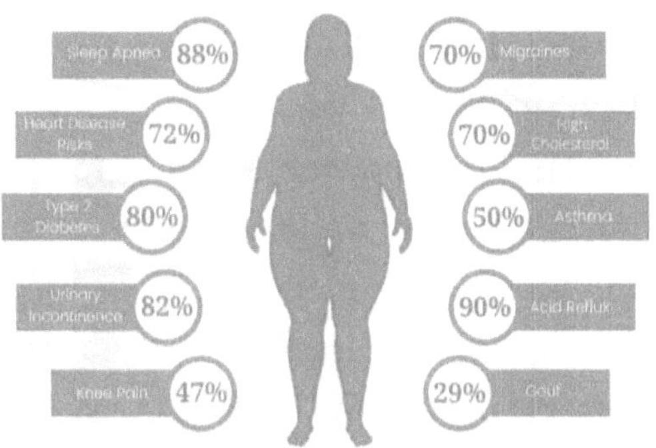

Obesity Related Health Problems

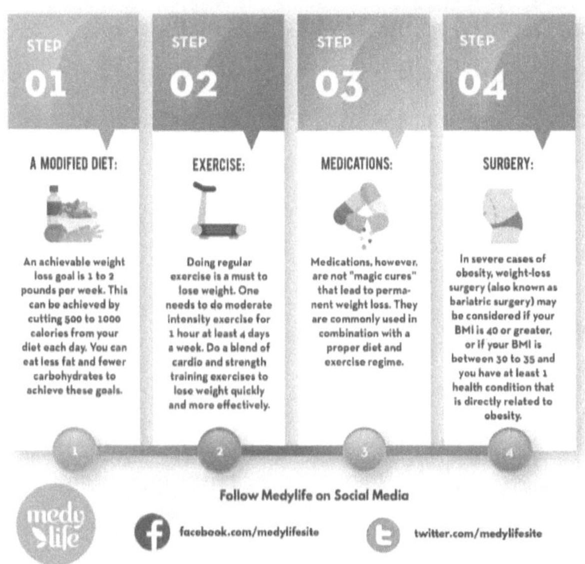

Step by Step Treatment to Obesity

6. PCOS – POLYCYSTIC OVARY SYNDROME

I) PCOS – FACTS

Polycystic ovary syndrome (PCOS) is a condition in which the ovaries produce an abnormal amount of androgens, male sex hormones that are usually present in women in small amounts. The name polycystic ovary syndrome describes the numerous small cysts (fluid-filled sacs) that form in the ovaries. However, some women with this disorder do not have cysts, while some women without the disorder do develop cysts.

Ovulation occurs when a mature egg is released from an ovary. This happens so it can be fertilized by a male sperm. If the egg is not fertilized, it is sent out of the body during the period.

In some cases, a woman doesn't make enough of the hormones needed to ovulate. When ovulation doesn't happen, the ovaries can develop many small cysts. These cysts make hormones called androgens. Women with PCOS often have high levels of androgens. This can cause more problems with a woman's menstrual cycle. And it can cause many of the symptoms of PCOS.

II) PCOS – KEY POINTS

- PCOS is a very common hormone problem for women of childbearing age.
- Women with PCOS may not ovulate, have high levels of androgens, and have many small cysts on the ovaries.
- PCOS can cause missed or irregular menstrual periods, excess hair growth, acne, infertility, and weight gain.

- Women with PCOS may be at higher risk for type 2 diabetes, high blood pressure, heart problems, and endometrial cancer.
- The types of treatment for PCOS may depend on whether or not a woman plans to become pregnant. Women who plan to become pregnant in the future may take different kinds of medications.

III) PCOS – CAUSES

The exact cause of PCOS is not clear. Many women with PCOS have insulin resistance. This means the body can't use insulin well. Insulin levels build up in the body and may cause higher androgen levels. Obesity can also increase insulin levels and make PCOS symptoms worse.

PCOS may also run in families. It's common for sisters or a mother and daughter to have PCOS.

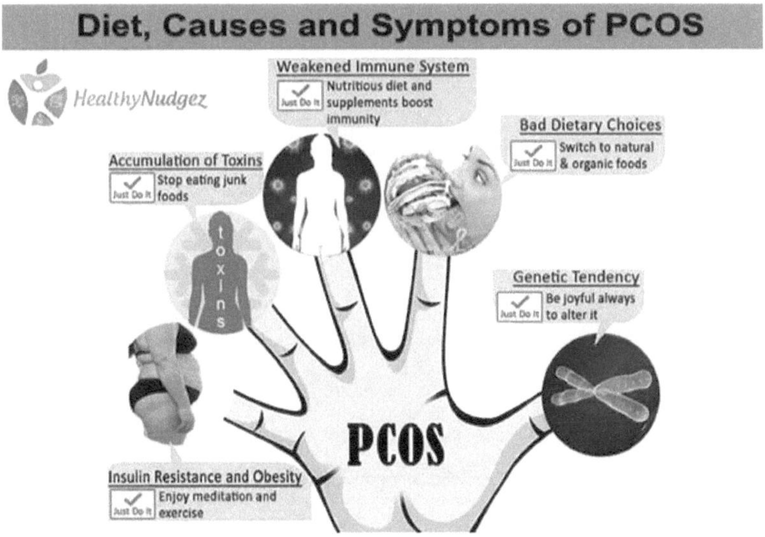

IV) PCOS – SYMPTOMS & COMPLICATIONS

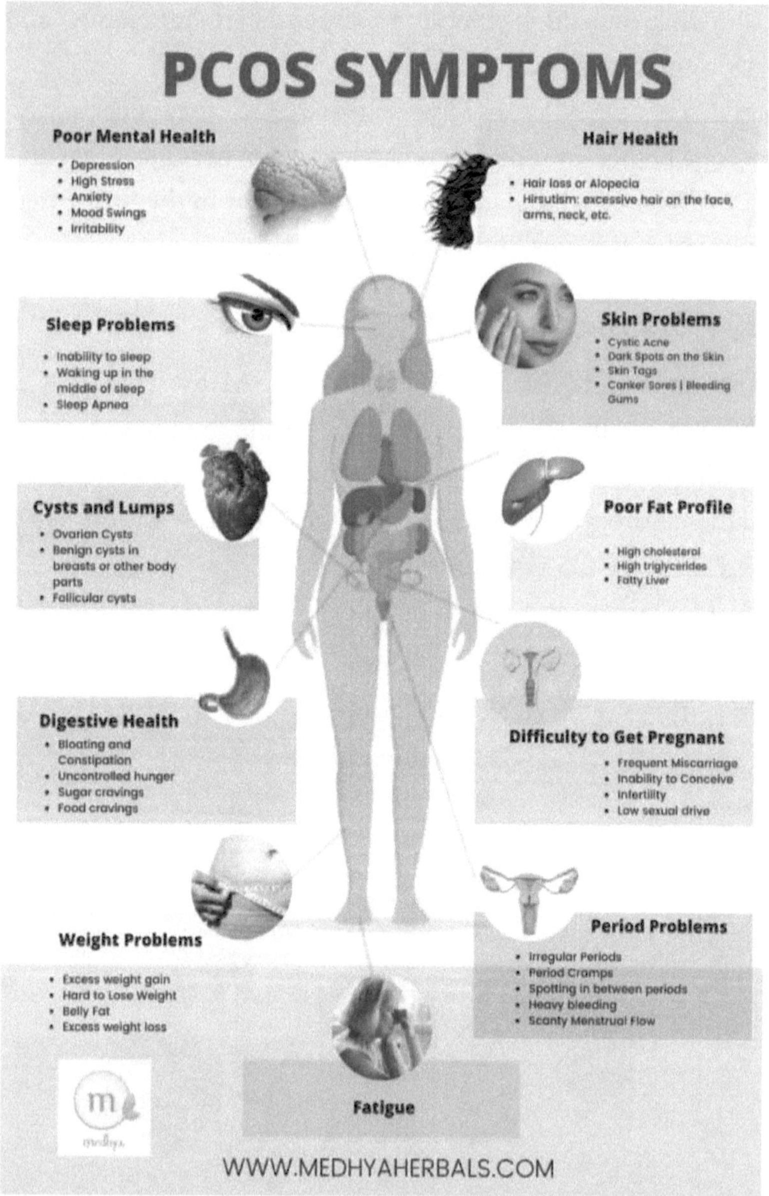

Women with PCOS are more likely to develop certain serious health problems. These include type 2 diabetes, high blood pressure, problems with the heart and blood vessels, and uterine cancer. Women with PCOS often have problems with their ability to get pregnant (fertility).

The symptoms of PCOS may include:
- Missed periods, irregular periods, or very light periods
- Ovaries that are large or have many cysts
- Excess body hair, including the chest, stomach, and back (hirsutism)
- Weight gain, especially around the belly (abdomen)
- Acne or oily skin
- Male-pattern baldness or thinning hair
- Infertility
- Small pieces of excess skin on the neck or armpits (skin tags)
- Dark or thick skin patches on the back of the neck, in the armpits, and under the breasts

V) PCOS – COMPLICATIONS – ITS AFFECT ON OUR BODY – INTERNALLY & EXTERNALLY

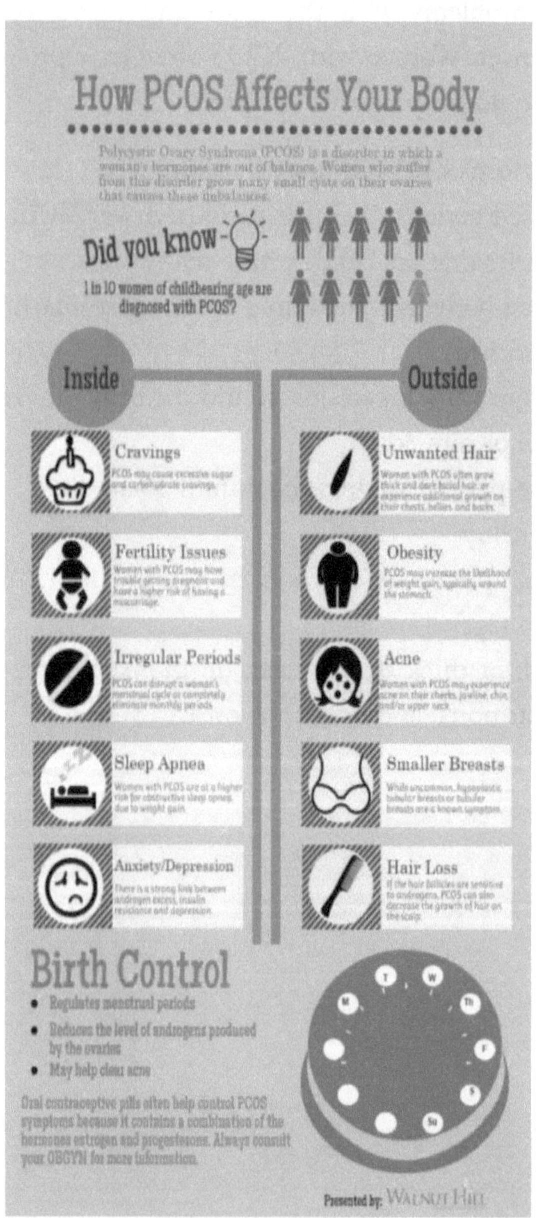

7. THYROID

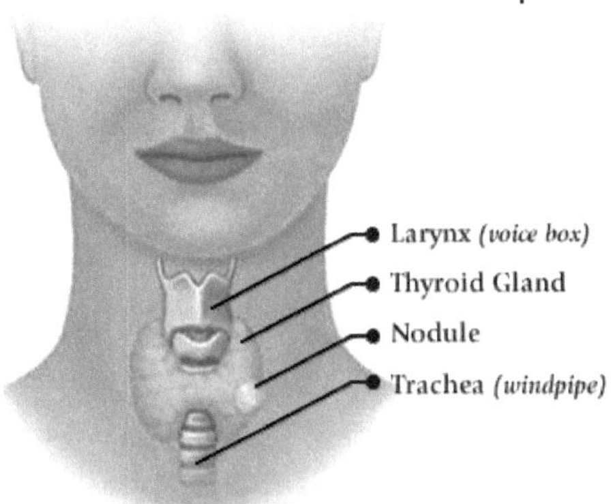

Thyroid Gland

- **Location**: below the larynx on each side of and anterior to the trachea
- **Size**: One of the largest endocrine glands
- **Weigh**: 5 to 20 grams in adults.
- **Secretions**: Thyroxine T4 and Triiodothyronine T3
- They increase metabolic rate of the body.
- Lack of thyroid secretion ⟶ basal metabolic rate 40 to 50 % below normal
- Excesses of thyroid secretion ⟶ 60 to 100% above normal.
- Thyroid secretion controlled TSH
- Thyroid gland also secretes calcitonin, hormone for calcium metabolism

The thyroid gland is a small organ that is located in the front of the neck, wrapped around the windpipe (trachea). It's shaped like a butterfly, smaller in the middle with two wide wings that extend around the side of our throat. This thyroid is a gland. We have glands throughout our body, where they create and release substances that help our body do a specific thing. Our thyroid makes hormones that helps to control many vital functions of our body.

THYROID FUNCTIONS GUIDE:

T3 (triiodothyronine), T4 (thyroxine), and TSH (thyroid-stimulating hormone) are important hormones produced by the thyroid gland. These hormones play a crucial role in regulating the body's metabolism, energy production, and overall growth and development.

Here's an interpretation of each of these thyroid hormones:

1. **T3 (Triiodothyronine):** T3 is the active form of thyroid hormone and is primarily responsible for regulating metabolism. It helps to control the rate at which the body uses energy, influences heart rate, and supports proper digestion. T3 is produced in smaller quantities compared to T4, but it is more potent.

   ➢ **Interpretation:**
     - Low T3 levels (hypothyroidism) can lead to symptoms like fatigue, weight gain, and sensitivity to cold.
     - High T3 levels (hyperthyroidism) can result in symptoms such as weight loss, rapid heartbeat, and nervousness.

2. **T4 (Thyroxine):** T4 is the precursor to T3 and is converted to active T3 in various tissues. It helps to regulate metabolism, growth, and body

temperature. T4 is produced in larger quantities by the thyroid gland.

> **Interpretation:**
> - Low T4 levels (hypothyroidism) can lead to similar symptoms as low T3 levels.
> - High T4 levels (hyperthyroidism) can cause symptoms similar to high T3 levels.

3. **TSH (Thyroid-Stimulating Hormone):** TSH is produced by the pituitary gland in response to the levels of T3 and T4 in the blood. It plays a role in controlling the thyroid gland's production of T3 and T4. If T3 and T4 levels are low, the pituitary gland releases more TSH to stimulate the thyroid gland to produce more hormones.

> **Interpretation:**
> - Low TSH levels often indicate hyperthyroidism, where the thyroid is producing excessive amounts of T3 and T4.
> - High TSH levels typically suggest hypothyroidism, where the thyroid is producing insufficient amounts of T3 and T4.

NOTE: It's important to note that interpreting these thyroid hormone levels should always be done by a medical professional. Thyroid disorders are complex and can have various underlying causes, so a comprehensive medical evaluation is necessary for accurate diagnosis and treatment.

What is the function of the thyroid gland into our bodies??

1: It takes Iodine from our food and convert it to T3 & T4 hormones.

2: It regulate many vital processes inside the body like :

a) Metabolism
b) Heart rate
c) Breathing
d) Cholesterol levels
e) Calcium levels and bone metabolism regulated by Calcitonin.

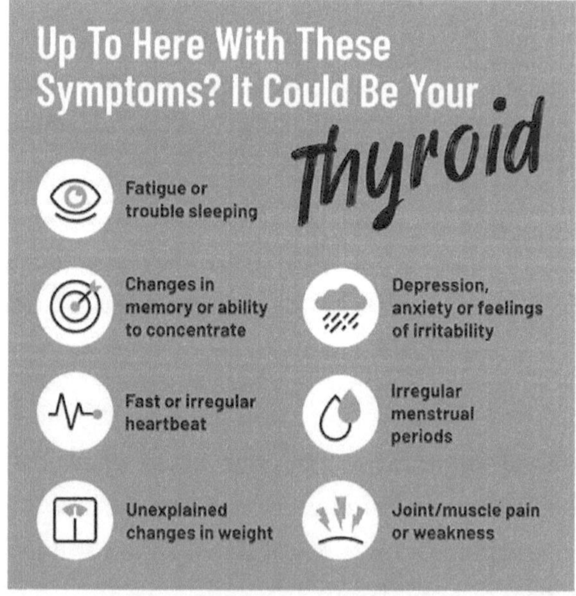

Symptoms of Thyroid

Thyroid has an important job to do within our body — releasing and controlling thyroid hormones that control metabolism. Metabolism is a process where the food we take into your body is transformed into energy. This energy is used throughout our entire body to keep many of our body's systems working correctly. Think of our metabolism as a generator. It takes in raw energy and uses it to power something bigger.

The thyroid controls our metabolism with a few specific hormones — **T4** (thyroxine, contains four iodide atoms) and **T3** (triiodothyronine, contains three iodide atoms). These two hormones are created by the thyroid and they tell the body's cells how much energy to use. When our thyroid works properly, it will maintain the right amount of hormones to keep our metabolism working at the right rate. As the hormones are used, the thyroid creates replacements.

This is all supervised by something called the **Pituitary gland**. Located in the centre of the skull, below our brain, the pituitary gland monitors and controls the amount of thyroid hormones in our bloodstream. When the pituitary gland senses a lack of thyroid hormones or a high level of hormones in our body, it will adjust the amounts with its own hormone. This hormone is called **Thyroid Stimulating Hormone – (TSH).** The TSH will be sent to the thyroid and it will tell the thyroid what needs to be done to get the body back to normal.

When our thyroid doesn't work properly, it can impact our entire body. If our body makes too much thyroid hormone, we can develop a condition called **Hyperthyroidism.** If our body makes too little thyroid hormone, it's called **Hypothyroidism.** Both conditions are serious and need to be treated by our healthcare provider.

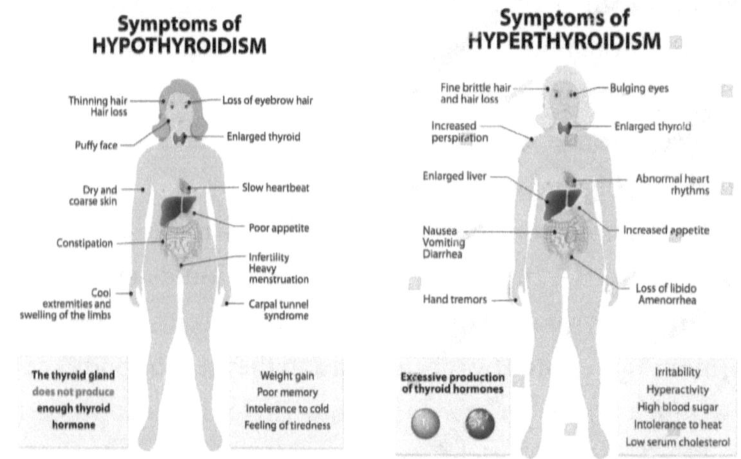

DIAGNOSIS AND TESTS

Sometimes, thyroid disease can be difficult to diagnose because the symptoms are easily confused with those of other conditions. One may experience similar symptoms when one is pregnant or aging and we would when, developing a thyroid disease. Fortunately, there are tests that can help determine if our symptoms are being caused by a thyroid issue. These tests include:

- Blood tests.
- Imaging tests.
- Physical exams.

BLOOD TESTS

- One of the most definitive ways to diagnose a thyroid problem is through blood tests. Thyroid blood tests are used to tell if our thyroid gland is functioning properly by measuring the amount of thyroid hormones in our blood. These tests are done by taking blood from a vein in our arm. Thyroid blood tests are used to see if we have – **Hyperthyroidism / Hypothyroidism.**

IMAGING TESTS

In many cases, taking a look at the thyroid itself can answer a lot of questions. Our healthcare provider might do an imaging test called a thyroid scan. This allows our health provider to look at our thyroid to check for an increased size, shape or growths (nodules).

PHYSICAL EXAM

Another way to quickly check the thyroid is with a physical test at your healthcare provider's clinic. This is a very simple and painless test where your provider feels your neck for any growths or enlargement of the thyroid.

REFERENCE RANGES OF T3, T4 AND TSH

Reference ranges for thyroid hormones T3 (triiodothyronine), T4 (thyroxine), and TSH (thyroid-stimulating hormone) can vary slightly depending on the laboratory and the specific assay methods they use. These ranges are usually determined by analysing a large sample of healthy individuals to establish what is considered normal for a particular population. Here are general reference ranges for these thyroid hormones:

1. **T3 (Triiodothyronine):**
   - Total T3: 80 – 200 ng/dL (nanograms per decilitre)
   - Free T3: 2.0 – 4.4 pg/mL (picograms per millilitre)
2. **T4 (Thyroxine):**
   - Total T4: 4.5 – 12.5 µg/dL (micrograms per decilitre)
   - Free T4: 0.8 – 2.8 ng/dL (nanograms per decilitre)
3. **TSH (Thyroid-Stimulating Hormone):**
   - 0.4 – 4.0 mIU/L (milli-international units per litre)
   - *There are separate reference ranges for children and pregnant women.

It's important to note that "normal" ranges can vary slightly between labs, and some labs might use slightly different units for measurement. Additionally, reference ranges can differ based on factors such as age, gender, and underlying health conditions.

When interpreting thyroid hormone levels, it's crucial to consider the context of the individual's health and medical history. Deviations from the reference range may indicate an underlying thyroid disorder. For example:

- **Hypothyroidism:** Low levels of T3 and T4, and high levels of TSH, are often indicative of an underactive thyroid gland.
- **Hyperthyroidism:** High levels of T3 and T4, and low levels of TSH, can suggest an overactive thyroid gland.

NOTE: It's important to work with a qualified healthcare professional to interpret these results accurately. They will consider the individual's symptoms, medical history, and overall health to make an informed diagnosis and recommend appropriate treatment if necessary. Regular monitoring of thyroid hormone levels is crucial for managing thyroid disorders and ensuring optimal thyroid function.

BODY STATISTICS FORMULAE & MEASUREMENTS

1. BMI – BODY MASS CALCULATOR

BMI is a measurement of a person's leanness or corpulence based on their height and weight, and is intended to quantify tissue mass. It is widely used as a general indicator of whether a person has a healthy body weight for their height.

Specifically, the value obtained from the calculation of BMI is used to categorize whether a person is underweight, normal weight, overweight, or obese depending on what range the value falls between.

These ranges of BMI vary based on factors such as region and age, and are sometimes further divided into subcategories such as severely underweight or very severely obese.

Being overweight or underweight can have significant health effects, so while BMI is an imperfect measure of healthy body weight, it is a useful indicator of whether any additional testing or action is required.

Refer to the table below to see the different categories based on BMI that is used by the calculator.

World Health Organisation – Body Mass Index (BMI) Range for Adults Above 18 Years

Category	BMI range – kg/m²
Severe Thinness	< 16
Moderate Thinness	16 – 17
Mild Thinness	17 – 18.5
Normal	18.5 – 25
Overweight	25 – 30
Obese Class I	30 – 35
Obese Class II	35 – 40
Obese Class III	> 40

BMI FORMULA

Below are the equations used for calculating BMI in the International System of Units (SI) of an individual as an example:

SI, Metric Units:

$$BMI = \frac{mass\ (kg)}{height^2\ (m)} = \frac{72.57}{1.78^2} = 22.90\ \frac{kg}{m^2}$$

BMI TABLE FOR ADULTS

This is the World Health Organization's (WHO) recommended body weight based on BMI values for adults. It is used for both men and women, age 18 or older.

LIMITATIONS OF BMI

Although BMI is a widely used and useful indicator of healthy body weight, it does have its limitations. BMI is only an estimate that cannot take body composition into account. Due to a wide variety of body types as well as distribution of muscle, bone mass, and fat, BMI should be considered along with other measurements rather than being used as the sole method for determining a person's healthy body weight.

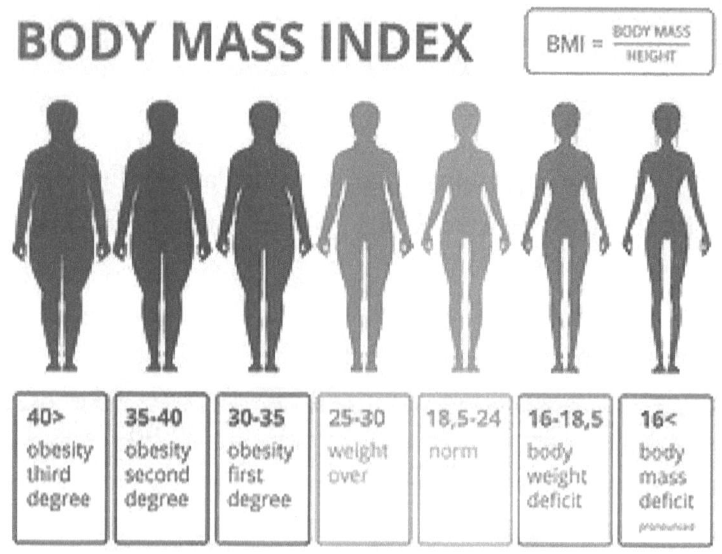

Pictorial Representation of BMI & Its Limits

BMI HEIGHT To WEIGHT AGE CHART in Kg & lbs

Height			Weight								
			Underweight		Normal		Overweight		Obese		Extreme Obese	
in	ft-in	cm	Kg	lbs	Kg	lbs	kg	lbs	kg	lbs	kg	lbs
58"	4ft 10"	147.3	35 - 40.2	77 - 89	40.2 - 52	91 - 115	54.5 - 63.6	119 - 138	65.9 - 84.1	143 - 185	88.6+	191+
59"	4ft 11"	149.9	36 - 41.5	79 - 94	41.5 - 54	94 - 119	56.2 - 65.2	124 - 143	68.2 - 88.6	148 - 193	90.9+	196+
60"	5ft	152.4	37.2 - 43	82 - 97	45.5 - 56.8	97 - 123	59.1 - 68.2	128 - 148	70.5 - 90.9	153 - 199	93.2 +	204+
61"	5ft 1"	154.9	38.5 - 45.5	85 - 100	45.5 - 59.1	100 - 127	61.4 - 70.5	132 - 153	72.7 - 93.2	158 - 206	96.5 +	211+
62"	5ft 2"	157.4	39.6 - 45.5	87 - 104	47.7 - 61.4	104 - 131	63.6 - 72.7	136 - 158	75.0 - 97.7	164 - 213	99.0+	218+
63"	5ft 3"	160	41.0 - 45.5	90 - 107	47.7 - 63.6	107 - 135	65.9 - 75.0	141 - 163	77.3 - 100	169 - 220	102.3+	225+
64"	5ft 4"	162.5	42.2 - 47.7	93 - 110	50.0 - 65.9	110 - 140	68.2 - 77.3	145 - 169	79.5 - 103	174 - 227	106.8+	232+
65"	5ft 5"	165.1	43.5 - 50.0	96 - 114	52.3 - 65.9	114 - 141	68.2 - 79.5	150 - 174	81.8 - 106.2	180 - 234	109.1+	240+
66"	5ft 6"	167.6	45.0 - 50.0	99 - 118	52.3 - 68.2	118 - 148	70.5 - 84.1	155 - 179	86.4 - 109.5	186 - 241	111.6+	247+
67"	5ft 7"	170.1	46.2 - 52.3	102 - 121	54.5 - 70.5	121 - 153	72.7 - 86.4	159 - 185	88.6 - 112.9	191 - 249	115.7+	255+
68"	5ft 8"	172.7	47.7 - 54.5	105 - 125	56.8 - 72.7	125 - 158	75.0 - 88.6	164 - 190	90.9 - 116.2	197 - 256	119.2+	262+
69"	5ft 9"	175.2	49 - 56.8	108 - 128	59.1 - 75.0	128 - 162	77.3 - 90.9	169 - 196	93.2 - 119.6	201 - 263	122.7+	270+
70"	5ft 10"	177.8	50.5 - 56.8	112 - 132	59.1 - 77.3	132 - 167	79.5 - 93.2	174 - 202	96.5 - 123.2	209 - 271	126.3+	278+
71"	5ft 11"	180.3	52 - 59.1	115 - 136	61.4 - 79.5	136 - 172	81.8 - 96.5	179 - 208	97.7 - 126.7	215 - 279	130+	286+
72"	6ft	182.8	53.3 - 61.4	118 - 140	63.6 - 81.8	140 - 177	84.1 - 100	184 - 213	102.3 - 130.2	221 - 287	133.5+	294+
73"	6ft 1"	185.4	55 - 61.4	121 - 144	63.6 - 84.1	144 - 182	86.4 - 102.3	189 - 219	104.5 - 134	227 - 295	137.5+	302+
74"	6ft 2"	187.9	56.5 - 63.6	125 - 148	65.9 - 86.4	148 - 186	88.6 - 104.5	194 - 225	106.8 - 137.6	233 - 303	141.1+	311+
75"	6ft 3"	190.5	58 - 65.9	128 - 152	68.2 - 88.6	152 - 192	90.9 - 106.8	200 - 232	109.1 - 141.4	240 - 311	145+	319+
76"	6ft 4"	193	59.5 - 69.5	131 - 154	70.5 - 90.9	156 - 197	93.2 - 107.9	205 - 238	111.6 - 145.2	246 - 320	149+	328+
BMI Ranges			16 - 18.5		18.5 - 24.9		25 - 29.9		30 - 39.9		Over 40	

Note : Age -In Medical Science, age shouldn't be a determinant of an BMI figure from middle age on-wards because the height of a human generally stays constant and does not go through the growth in height apparent in young ages.

2. BODY FAT CALCULATOR

BMI METHOD:

The estimation of BMI involves the use of formulas that require the measurement of a person's height and weight.

Given BMI, the following formulas can be used to estimate a person's body fat percentage.

   i. **Body fat percentage (BFP) formula for adult males:**

$$BFP = 1.20 \times BMI + 0.23 \times Age - 16.2$$

   ii. **Body fat percentage (BFP) formula for adult females:**

$$BFP = 1.20 \times BMI + 0.23 \times Age - 5.4$$

   iii. **Body fat percentage (BFP) formula for boys:**

$$BFP = 1.51 \times BMI - 0.70 \times Age - 2.2$$

   iv. **Body fat percentage (BFP) formula for girls:**

$$BFP = 1.51 \times BMI - 0.70 \times Age + 1.4$$

The Body Mass Index (BMI) Calculator can be used to calculate BMI value and corresponding weight status while taking age into consideration. Use the "Metric Units" tab for the International System of Units or the "Other Units" tab to convert units into either US or metric units.

Jackson & Pollard Ideal Body Fat Percentages of Men & Women – Age Wise

Age	Women	Men
20	17.7%	8.5%
25	18.4%	10.5%
30	19.3%	12.7%
35	21.5%	13.7%
40	22.2%	15.3%
45	22.9%	16.4%
50	25.2%	18.9%
55	26.3%	20.9%

WHAT IS BODY FAT PERCENTAGE

Body fat is the amount of fat present in our body, apart from everything else including your muscles, tendons, bones and our organs – the stomach, kidney, liver, brain, etc.

Body fat can be further classified into two categories: **Essential Fat and Storage Fat**.

Essential Fat is the fat which is required for healthy functioning of the body. *The amount of essential fat in a male is approximately*

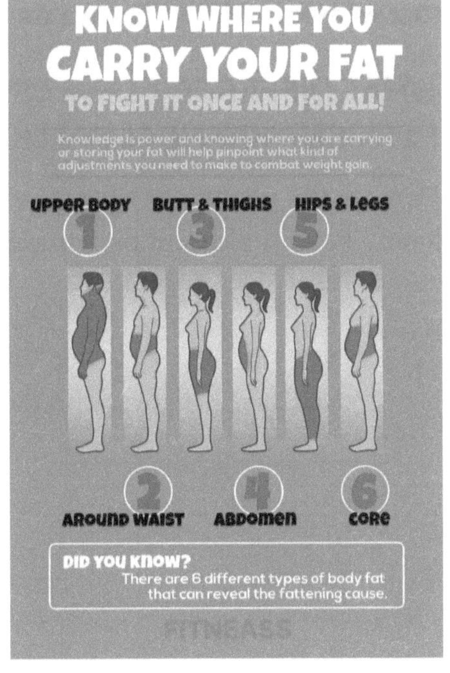

3% of the body weight. On the other hand, *females have a high percentage of essential fat – about 12%.*

Anything less than this level of body fat can prove fatal for the body and worst – organ failure.

It is because of this very reason that all the *bodybuilders keep a higher body fat levels throughout the year* and cut down only when they need to get ready for the show.

Storage fat, as the name suggests, is the type of fat that we store beneath our skin and muscles. This fat is responsible for protecting our internal organs from injuries.

Although storage fat is important for the body, too much of it can lead to excess weight gain. So, **it is this storage fat that we want to lose when we want to lose weight.**

WHAT DIFFERENT LEVELS OF BODY FAT PERCENTAGE REALLY LOOKS LIKE?

Here are few pictures of what an adult men and women really looks like with different percentage of body fat:

Calculate BMI first using above formula and then calculate BFP applying formula. Now compare the calculated % figures with the images represented below.

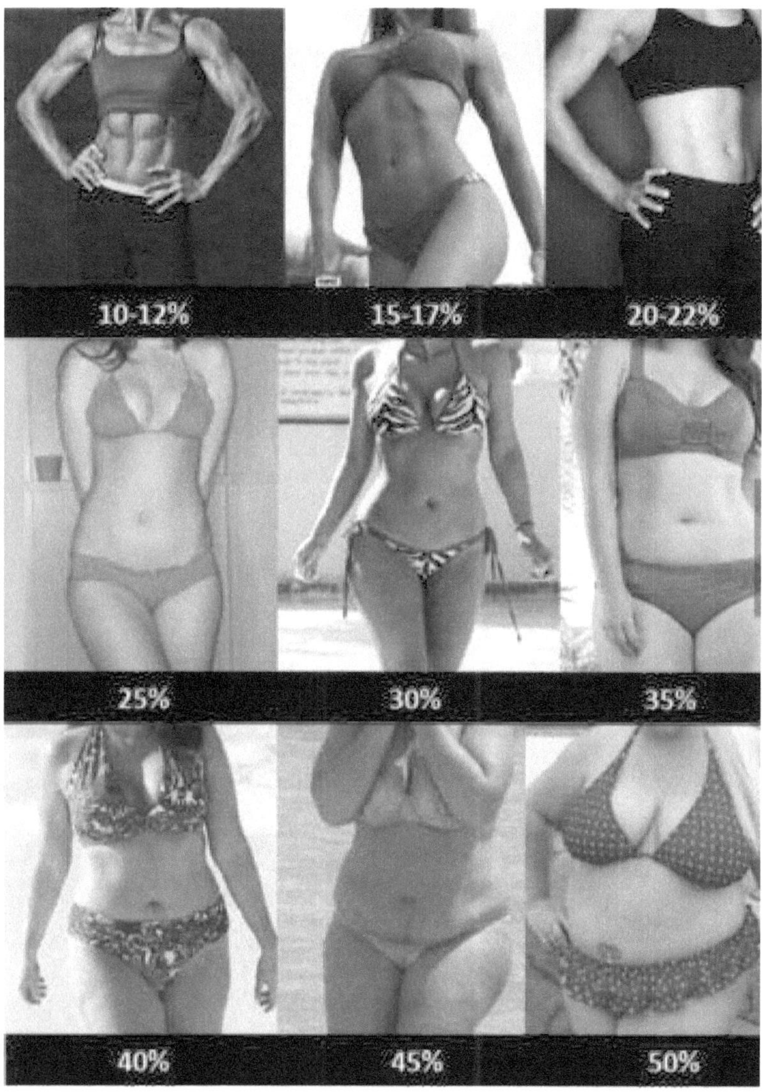

Pictorial view of an ADULT FEMALE – % of BODY FAT

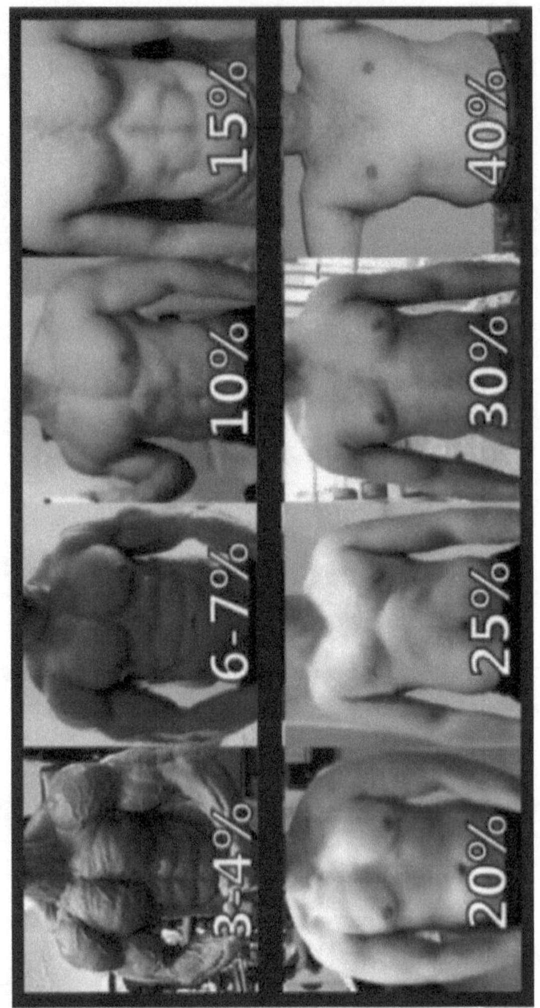

Pictorial view of an ADULT MALE – % of BODY FAT

IMPORTANT NOTE: These visual pictorial images of an adult male and female are only for the purpose of visually indicating the physical stature of the portions of the human body, depicting the different percentage levels of STORAGE FATS present in our body, and how truly a person looks alike.

BALANCED DIET FOR A HEALTHY LIFESTYLE

1. COMPONENTS OF A BALANCED DIET

1. VITAMINS AND MINERALS

These are body protecting nutrients. They regulate body metabolism and protect against infections, deficiency diseases and any metabolic imbalances.

Make sure to include multi-coloured, whole fruits and vegetables that are a treasure of minerals and vitamins.

Food & Vegetables provide key nutrients that keep us healthy. Similarly, vegetables such as dark green leafy veggies should be included in our meal. Adding a variety of **fresh green leafy veggies** to our meal will help us in getting the bountiful nutrients required for the body.

2. PROTEIN

This nutrient is associated with bodybuilding, growth, and development. This is required to help our body repair cells and make new ones.

According to Harvard Medical School about 20% of your daily diet should consist of protein found in pulses like **whole grams, dals, chickpeas, peas, lentils, beans, peanuts, milk, eggs, fish, and meat.**

Protein also plays an important role in growth and development during the early stages of childhood, adolescence, and pregnancy.

3. CARBOHYDRATE

This nutrient is equally necessary as associated with energy giving and sustainability. The voluntary and involuntary functions of the body are well-regulated with the efficient supply of energy in the form of glucose.

Consume complex carbohydrates which inclide whole grains such as **rice, wheat, ragi, jowar, bajra, oatmeal, quinoa, and potatoes** among others. Hence, carbs should not be avoided and it should be a part of our daily diet.

4. FATS

Fats play an important role in providing energy, circulation of vitamins and hormone synthesis. Include more of a beneficial fat, which are high in unsaturated fatty acids like **MUFA** – (Monosaturated fatty acids) and **PUFA** – (Polysaturated fatty acids) that provides essential fatty acids as in **sunflower oil, fish oil, nuts and seeds.**

TYPE OF ESSENTIAL VITAMINS & MAJOR MINERALS & THEIR FUNCTIONS

I) FAT SOLUABLE VITAMIN

- Vitamin A
- Vitamin D
- Vitamin E
- Vitamin K

FUNCTIONS:

Together this vitamin quartet helps to keep our eyes, skin, lungs, gastrointestinal tract, and nervous system in good functioning condition. Here are some of the other essential roles these vitamins play:

Build bones. Bone formation would be impossible without vitamins A, D, and K.

Protect vision. Vitamin A also helps to keep cells healthy and protects our vision.

Interact favourably. Without vitamin E, our body would have difficulty in absorbing and storing vitamin A.

Protect the body. Vitamin E also acts as an antioxidant (a compound that helps to protect the body against damage from unstable molecules).

II) WATER-SOLUBLE VITAMINS – [VITAMIN B & C]

Water-soluble vitamins are packed into the watery portions of the foods we eat. They are absorbed directly into the bloodstream, as food is broken down during digestion or as a supplement dissolves.

Because much of our body consists of water, many of the water-soluble vitamins circulate easily in our body. Our kidneys continuously regulate levels of water-soluble vitamins, shunting excesses out of the body in our urine.

Vitamin 'B'
- Biotin (vitamin B7)
- Folic acid (folate, vitamin B9)

- Niacin (vitamin B3)
- Pantothenic acid (vitamin B5)
- Riboflavin (vitamin B2)
- Thiamin (vitamin B1)
- Vitamin B6
- Vitamin B12 **&**

Vitamin 'C'

FUNCTIONS:

Although water-soluble vitamins have many tasks in the body, one of the most important is helping to free the energy found in the food we eat. Others help to keep tissues healthy. Here are some examples of how different vitamins help us to maintain health:

- **Release energy:** Several B vitamins are key components of certain co-enzymes (molecules that aid enzymes) that helps to release energy from the food.
- **Produce energy:** Thiamin, Riboflavin, Niacin, Pantothenic acid, and Biotin engage in energy production.
- **Build proteins and cells:** Vitamins B6, B12, and folic acid metabolize amino acids (the building blocks of proteins) and help the cells to multiply.
- **Make collagen.** One of the many roles played by vitamin C is to help to make **collagen** (A protein molecule made up of amino acids and it provides structural support to the extracellular space of

connective tissues) which knits together wounds, supports blood vessel walls, and forms a base for teeth and bones.

III) MAJOR MINERALS

Major minerals travel through the body in various ways. Potassium, for example, is quickly absorbed into the bloodstream, where it circulates freely and is excreted by the kidneys, much like a water-soluble vitamin. Calcium is more like a fat-soluble vitamin because it requires a carrier for absorption and transport.

Major minerals
- Calcium
- Chloride
- Magnesium
- Phosphorus
- Potassium
- Sodium
- Sulphur

FUNCTIONS:

One of the key tasks of major minerals is to maintain the proper balance of water in the body. Sodium, chloride, and potassium take the lead in doing this. Three other major minerals—calcium, phosphorus, and magnesium—are important for healthy bones. Sulphur helps to stabilize protein structures, including some of those that make up hair, skin, and nails.

2. TEN AMAZING WAYS TO MAINTAIN A BALANCED DIET CHART

1. FOLLOW THE CORRECT MEALTIME

A diet chart comprises of 5 small meals in a day with a gap of 3 hours between each meal. A gap of more than 3 hours will increase the stress hormones cortisol that will let the body store fat in the belly.

If these meals are eaten in proper time, it will keep the cortisol levels in check and thus reducing belly fat. Food eaten at the right time will also help in better digestion.

An irregular eating pattern affects the metabolism and can even hinder the normal cardiometabolic health.

2. BE PHYSICALLY ACTIVE DURING THE DAY

If we are physically active during the day, it will help us in reducing weight and we will feel less lethargic. Diet alone is not sufficient when it comes to achieving ideal health. With the input of calories, it is essential for its release as well so as to maintain the balance.

If we are inactive and lacking in physical activity than our body might accumulate extra calories that is harmful in the long run.

3. MAINTAIN A LIST OF HEALTHY FOODS

Research and gather knowledge about the foods and their nutrient content. This will give us an idea of the foods that are nutritious and meeting our health requirements.

4. REPLACE PROCESSED FOODS WITH FRUITS AND VEGGIES

Fresh fruits and leafy vegetables are the natural foods that will help to maintain a healthy diet chart for the body. Sadly, these foods have been replaced by processed foods.

For example, tinned vegetables or breakfast cereals being the main culprit for weight gain. Similarly, prefer having whole fruits rather than consuming market available fruit juices.

Processed foods are unhealthy and contain added sugar, salt, and fat. They also contain preservatives and additives that can lead to life-threatening consequences like cancer. **Therefore, prefer more fruits, vegetables, and specially home-cooked food.**

5. INCLUDE MORE PROTEINS

If we want to lose weight, add more proteins to our diet, as protein takes more time and energy to break down in the body. **Protein intake of 0.8-1 gram per kg body weight helps in weight loss** and maintaining healthy muscle mass as well.

We can include snacks like sprouts, peanuts, Greek yogurt and seeds instead of chips to fulfil our protein requirement.

For e.g. shake-a-day, a whey protein drink, a fruit pudding or quinoa can be eaten instead of rice.

6. INCLUDE MILK AND MILK PRODUCTS

Dairy products are the best source of calcium that is essential for healthy bones and is also necessary for regulating muscle contraction. If our calcium intake is inadequate, we might suffer from osteoporosis and various bone diseases.

Dairy products that are rich in calcium are low-fat yogurt, cottage cheese, and milk.

7. HAVE THE REQUIRED CARBS

It is wise to choose the required amount of carbs needed for the body. Most of the carbohydrates are present in plant foods like pulses, cereals, and millets.

Our healthy diet chart should mainly consist of complex carbohydrates such as whole grains, brown rice, oats, lentils, fruits, and vegetables.

They are rich in fibre which keeps us feeling fuller for a longer period of time. Researches have proved that regular intake of fibre ensures healthy prevention of metabolic disorders like diabetes, hypertension and cardiovascular diseases.

8. REDUCE THE FAT INTAKE

Decrease the intake of fats, specifically the one rich in saturated fats, as too much of it can lead to weight gain and other related health problems. For example, butter, margarine and solid fats.

The required amount of fats needed for the body totally depends on the foods that we are consuming. According to the Indian Council of Medical Research, the fat requirement for an adult man and woman is around 20 grams.

While cooking, we can go for refined or cold pressed oil which has a higher nutritional value than the unrefined oil.

9. CUT DOWN SUGAR IN YOUR TEA/COFFEE

Sugar is the lead villain to increase your waistline in the body. Sugar is addictive like a drug to most of the people, who like to add sweet sugar to their favourite foods.

Too much consumption of sugar may cause diabetes, insulin resistance, heart disease and obesity among many other lifestyle disorders.

10. REMOVE 'SALT' FROM THE TABLE

Eating too much salt, causes the extra water to store in our body that raises the blood pressure. According to a review published by Harvard School of Public Health, the excess intake of salt and sodium has a negative health impact on our heart, arteries, kidneys, and brain.

This can lead to heart attacks, strokes, dementia, and kidney disease. Also, sodium due to excess salt causes water retention that makes our body fluffy and heavy.

With the change in requirements and according to the pattern and customization of balanced diet chart, there is a variation among men and women diet chart also, as represented below:

RECOMMENDED BALANCED DIET CHART FOR MEN		
Meal	**Function**	**Comprises of**
Breakfast	Boost up the metabolism, provide satiety value	Veg poha with eggs or chila with chutney or khichdi /upma with veggies and sprouts salad
Mid-morning snack	Reduce the meal gap, provide essential nutrients, prevent hunger	Nuts and seeds / a fruit bowl with nuts
Lunch	Regulate blood sugar level, helps in improving focus and activity level	Rice with dal, chicken / paneer / sandwich topped with chicken / fish with plenty of salads
Mid-evening snack	Keep energy levels up, Reduce the meal gap, prevent hunger	Avocado salad / Apple cinnamon granola bar
Dinner	Overnight growth and repair, Body's functional sustainability	A bowl of cooked quinoa with chicken curry and lightly sauteed veggies / roti with veggies & dal soup / chicken soup

FOR MEN

RECOMMENDED BALANCED DIET CHART FOR WOMEN

Meal	Function	Comprises of
Breakfast	Boost up the metabolism, provide satiety value	2-3 scrambled egg whites with a whole grain toast and a fruit of your choice / a bowl of fruit oats porridge with sprouts salad
Mid-morning snack	Reduce the meal gap, provide essential nutrients, prevent hunger	A fistful of dried fruit combined with nuts or seeds
Lunch	Regulate blood sugar level, helps in improving focus and activity level	A bowl of dal/chicken/fish curry with brown rice / roti and a veg salad
Mid-evening snack	Keep energy levels up, Reduce the meal gap, prevent hunger	Apple cinnamon granola bar / Nature Valley's granola bar / you can have a fistful of nuts
Dinner	Overnight growth and repair, Body's functional sustainability	A bowl of Chicken / fish / paneer with roti / chila / quinoa preparations and soup or salad with veggies

FOR WOMEN

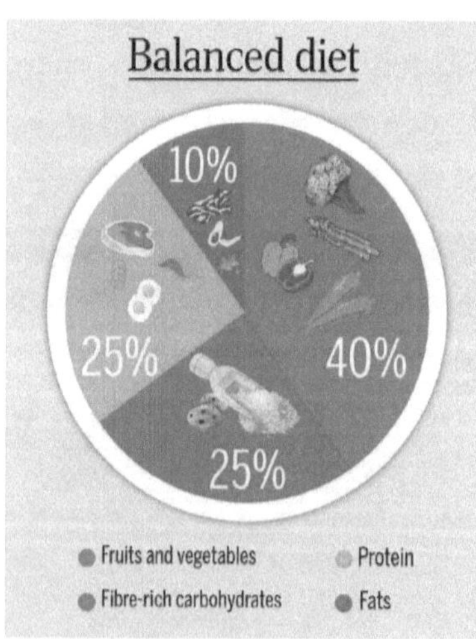

Proportionate Balanced Diet – %

Body weight	Water
45 kgs	1.9 Ltrs.
50 kgs	2.1 Ltrs.
55 kgs	2.3 Ltrs.
60 kgs	2.5 Ltrs.
65 kgs	2.7 Ltrs.
70 kgs	2.9 Ltrs.
75 kgs	3.2 Ltrs.
80 kgs	3.5 Ltrs.
85 kgs	3.7 Ltrs.
90 kgs	3.9 Ltrs.
95 kgs	4.1 Ltrs.
100 kgs	4.3 Ltrs.

Daily In-take Water Quantity as Per Body Weight

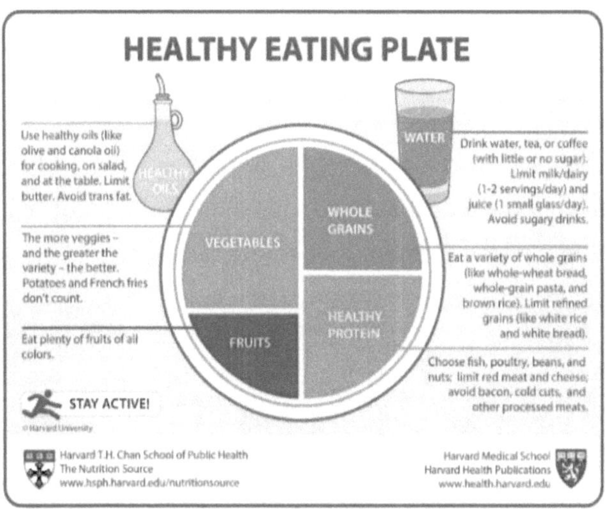

Main Constituents of a Balance Healthy Eating Plate

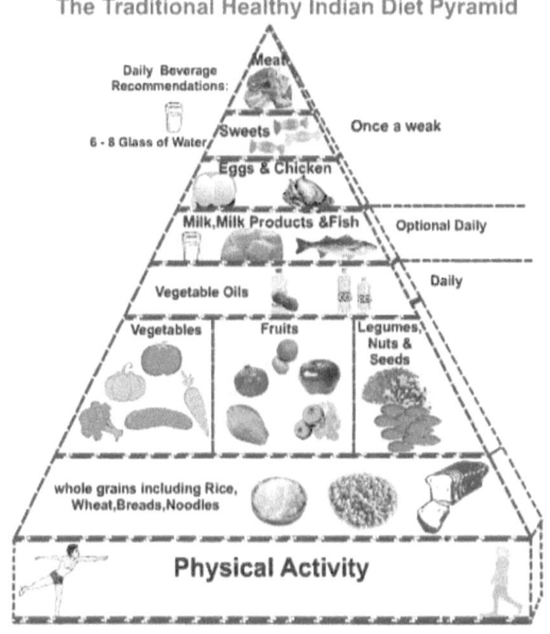

The Traditional Healthy Indian Diet Pyramid

ACCORDING TO INDIAN TRADITION – REGULAR CONSUMPTION OF FOOD ITEMS & ITS CALORIE VALUE: As per one's diet in-take, the calorie count can be added before/after consumption and estimated the total in-take calorie count and accordingly manage to achieve a target for opting a well-balanced diet on regular basis.

Calorie Sheet			
Sr. No.	Food Item	Quantity	Caloric Value
1	Boiled Egg	1	125
2	Egg Fried	1	110
3	Egg Omelette	1	120
4	Bread slice with butter	1	90
5	Chapati	1	60
6	Puri	1	75
7	Paratha	1	150
8	Subji	1 Cup	150
9	Idli	1	100
10	Dosa Plain	1	120
11	Dosa Masala	1	250
12	Sambhar	1 Cup	150
13	Cooked Rice - Plain	1 Cup	120
14	Cooked Rice - Fried	1 Cup	150
15	Phulka	1	60
16	Nan	1	150
17	Dal	1 Cup	150
18	Curd	1 Cup	100
19	Curry, Vegetable	1 Cup	150
20	Curry, Meat	1 Cup	175

3. VITAMIN CHART OF HEALTHY FOODS TO MAINTAIN A BALANCED DIET FOR BODY FUNCTIONS

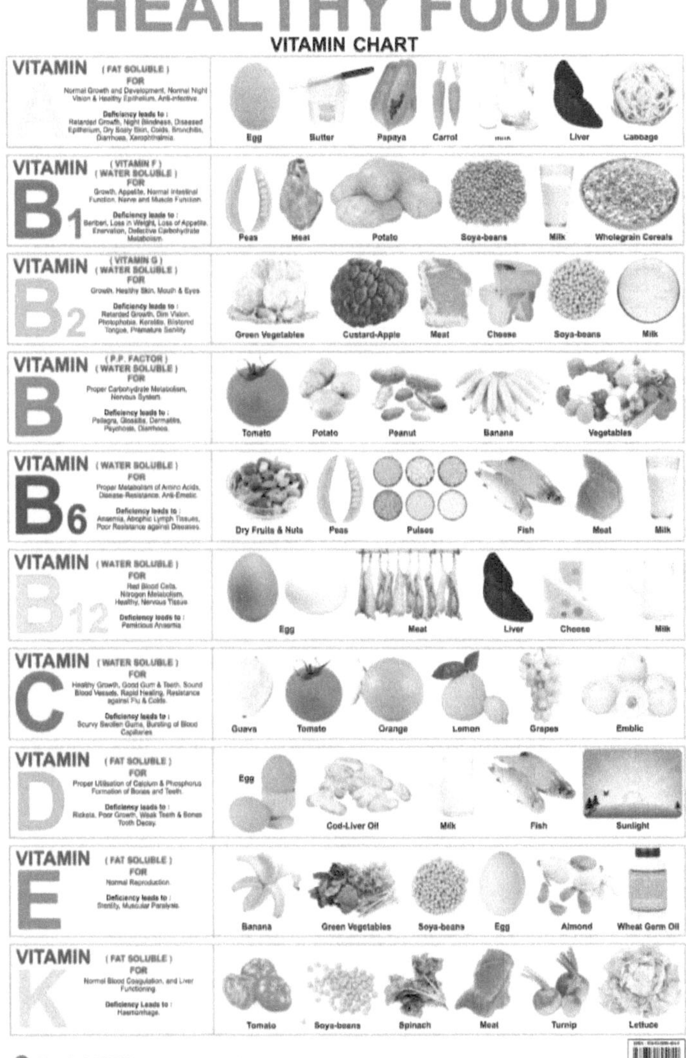

4. DETAILED CHART OF THE "13" VITAL VITAMINS REQUIRED FOR A COMPLETE BALANCED DIET

SR.NO.	VITAMIN	ALT. NAME	1 - MAIN FUNCTIONS
	VITAL VITAMIN - B COMPLEX		
1	B1	Thiamin	Converts protein, carbs & fat from food into energy, nervous system functions, synthesisi of DNA
2	B2	Riboflavin	Converts protein, carbs & fat from food into energy, skin health & eye health.
3	B3	Niacin	Converts protein, carbs & fat from food into energy, fatty acid synthesis & improves cholesterol
4	B5	Patothenic Acid	Converts carbs & fat from food into energy, production of red blood cells healthy digestion & hormone prodn.
5	B6	Pyroxidine	Protein & amino acid metabolism, release of stored glucose, brain functions & hormone production
6	B7	Biotin	Converts protein into energy, carb metabolism, fat synthesis, hair & nail health.
7	B9	Folic Acid	Protein & amino acid metabolism, DNA synthesis, formation of red blood cells.
8	B12	Cobalamin	Food metabolism & energy production DNA synthesis,formation of red blood cells, brain & nervous system functions
9	C		It is a powerfull antioxidant, it is used for the synthesis of collagen - a protein that supports healthy growth/repair of blood vessels, tendons, ligament & scar tissue. Improves iron absorption from food & boost immune system, controls com.cold
10	A	Retinoids & Carotenoids	It supports vision, healthy skin & teeth immunity, reproduction, organ function, cell growth.
11	D		Important for absorption of calcium, which helps maintain strong teeth & bones. Protects body, rejuvenate & maintain healthy skin cells & supports nerve, muscle & immune functions.
12	E		Like A&C, vitamin E is a potent antioxidant It safeguards stored fatty acids (PUFA's) from oxygen damage, also fights general diseases & inflammation, protects cells against free radicals.
13	K		Primarily helps with proper blood clotting - (or coagulation) which prevents excessive bleeding. Its also important for bone density, overall bone health & cell growth.

2 - BEST SOURCE	3 - DEFICIENCY
Cereal, spirulina, beans & lentils, flax seeds & other seeds, milk, nuts, oats, rice & wheat	Fatigue Nerve & brain damage Leads to beriberi
Milk, dairy products, egg, fish, green leafy veggies, cereals, whole grain & liver	Cracks in the lips Tongue swelling & other skin diseases. Leads to arbiflavinosis
Yeast, meat, fish, eggs, milk & dairy products, green vegetables, beans, nuts & cereal grains	Muscular weakness Loss of appetite Leads to pellagra
Fresh meat, vegetables & unprocessed grains	N/A
Liver, meat, fish, poultry, beans, wheat germ, bananas, legumes & cereal	Muscle weakness, Anxiety, Depression
Eggs, nuts, fish, nut butter, beans, whole grains, cauliflower, bananas & mushroom	Loss of appetite, Vomiting, Depression
Grain, bread, cereal, vegetables, beans, oranges & bananas.	GI pain Anemia
Liver, yogurt, dairy products, fish, oysters, non fat dry milk, salmon, sardines & clams	Nerve damage, Fatigue, Anemia
Most of the fruits & green veggies, Guava, peaches, kiwi, cauliflower, sprouts, lemon, oranges, grapes, lychee & strawberry	Fatigue, gum inflammation issues with wound healing & joint pain.
All orange & dark green veggies, kale, carrot, pumpkin, spinach, lettuce, tomatoes & brocolli	Diarrhea, vision issue & blindness & increased risk of infections.
Mainly from Sunlight, fish & dairy Milk, yogurt, egg, salmon, oysters, sardines, tuna, cod liver oil & cereals.	Weak bones - leads to rickets in children & osteoporosis in adults.
All types of nuts, seeds & oil, wheat germ, cereal, veggie oils, green leafy vegetables.	Nerve & muscle damage, weakened immunity & vision problems.
Primarly green leafy vegetables, Kale, collard greens, spinach, watercress, broccoli & brussels sprouts.	Bruising & bleeding, Osteoporosis.

5. CALORIE CALCULATOR

The *Calorie Calculator* can be used to estimate the number of calories a person needs to consume each day. This calculator can also provide some simple guidelines for gaining or losing weight.

BASAL METABOLIC RATE: Also known as **BMR.** Basal Metabolic Rate (BMR) is the amount of energy (calories) our body needs to maintain basic functions while at rest. It's the energy required to keep our body functioning, such as breathing, circulating blood, and regulating body temperature. There are different formulas to calculate BMR, with the Harris-Benedict equation being one of the most commonly used.

Here's how to calculate BMR using the Harris-Benedict equation:

For **Men: BMR = 88.362 + (13.397** × weight in kg) + **(4.799** × height in cm) − **(5.677** × age in years)

For **Women: BMR = 447.593 + (9.247** × weight in kg) + **(3.098** × height in cm) − **(4.330** × age in years)

Please note that the measurements for weight should be in kilograms, height in centimetres, and age in years.

To calculate your BMR using the Harris-Benedict equation:

1. Convert your weight from pounds to kilograms (divide by 2.205) and your height from inches to centimetres (multiply by 2.54), if necessary.
2. Plug your weight, height, and age into the appropriate formula based on your gender.
3. The result will be your BMR in calories per day.

Keep in mind that **BMR provides an estimate of your basic energy needs at rest.** To determine your total daily calorie needs, you'll need to consider your activity level. The Harris-Benedict equation offers different activity multipliers that you can use to estimate your total daily calorie expenditure:

- **Sedentary** (little to no exercise): **BMR × 1.2**
- **Lightly active** (light exercise/sports 1-3 days/week): **BMR × 1.375**
- **Moderately active** (moderate exercise/sports 3-5 days/week): **BMR × 1.55**
- **Very active** (hard exercise/sports 6-7 days a week): **BMR × 1.725**
- **Extremely active** (very hard exercise/sports, physical job, or training twice a day): **BMR × 1.9**

Remember that individual factors like genetics, muscle mass, and metabolism can influence BMR. Calculating BMR can give you a general idea of your daily calorie needs, but it's important to listen to your body's cues and adjust your intake based on your health and goals. If you're aiming for weight management, consider consulting with a healthcare professional or a registered dietitian for personalized guidance.

Daily calorie needs based on age, gender, and activity level

Age (Years)	Gender	Sedentary (Not Active)	Moderately Active	Active
2-3	Male or female	1,000	1,000	1,000
4-8	Male	1,200 – 1,400	1,400 – 1,600	1,600 – 2,000
	Female	1,200 – 1,400	1,400 – 1,600	1,400 – 1,800
9-13	Male	1,600 – 2,000	1,800 – 2,200	2,000 – 2,600
	Female	1,400 – 1,600	1,600 – 2,000	1,800 – 2,200
14-18	Male	2,000 – 2,400	2,400 – 2,800	2,800 – 3,200
	Female	1,800	2,000	2,400
19-30	Male	2,400 – 2,600	2,600 – 2,800	3,000
	Female	1,800 – 2,000	2,000 – 2,200	2,400
31-50	Male	2,200 – 2,400	2,400 – 2,600	2,800 – 3,000
	Female	1,800	2,000	2,200
51 and older	Male	2,000 – 2,200	2,200 – 2,400	2,400 – 2,800
	Female	1,600	1,800	2,000 – 2,200

Adapted from US Department of Agriculture and US Department of Health and Human Services. *Dietary Guidelines for Americans, 2010.* 7th ed. Washington, DC US Government Printing Office 2010. Http://www.health.gov/dietaryguidelines/2010.asp. Accessed March 18, 2014

Daily Calorie Needs Reqd. by Our Body – Based on Age, Gender & Activity Level.

E

OPTIMAL SLEEP THERAPY

1. ADVANTAGES OF OPTIMAL SLEEP THERAPY

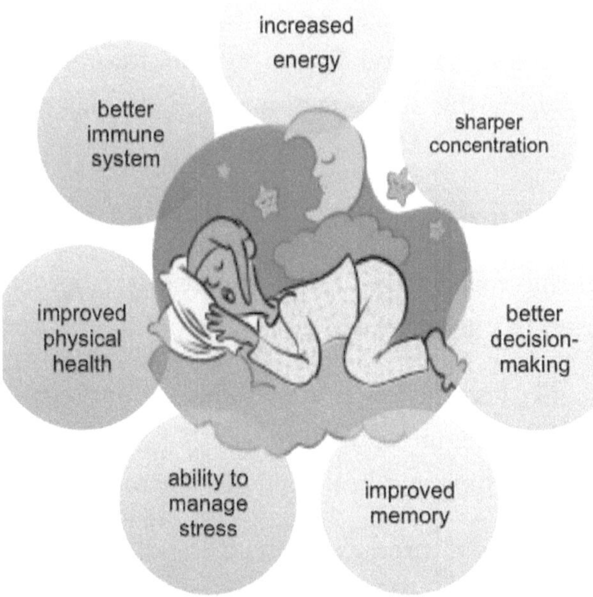

There are two main types of sleep:

a. **Non-rapid eye movement (NREM)**, also known as quiet sleep

b. **Rapid eye movement (REM)**, also known as active sleep or paradoxical sleep

A) NON-RAPID EYE MOVEMENT (NREM), ALSO KNOWN AS QUIET SLEEP

NREM STAGE 1 – ENTERING SLEEP

During the earliest phases of sleep, we are still relatively awake and alert.

Stage 1 is the beginning of the sleep cycle and is a relatively light stage of sleep. It can be considered a transition period between wakefulness and sleep.

In Stage 1, the brain produces high amplitude theta waves, which are very slow brain waves. This period of sleep lasts only a brief time (around five to 10 minutes). If we awake someone during this stage, they might report that they were not really asleep.

NREM STAGE 2

Stage 2 is the second stage of sleep and lasts for approximately 20 minutes. During stage 2 sleep:

- We become less aware of our surroundings.
- Body temperature drops.
- Breathing and heart rate become more regular.

The brain begins to produce bursts of rapid, rhythmic brain wave activity known as sleep spindles. Body temperature starts to decrease and heart rate begins to slow. According to the American Sleep Foundation, people spend approximately 50% of their total sleep in this stage.

NREM STAGE 3

During stage 3 sleep:

- Muscles relax.
- Blood pressure and breathing rate drop.
- Deepest sleep occurs.

Deep, slow brain waves known as delta waves begin to emerge during stage 3 sleep. This stage is also sometimes referred to as delta sleep.

During this stage, people become less responsive to noises and activity around in the environment and may fail to generate a response. It also acts as a transitional period between light sleep and a very deep sleep.

During the deep stages of NREM sleep, the body repairs and regrows tissues, builds bone and muscle, and strengthens the immune system.

Older studies suggested that bed-wetting was most likely to occur during this deep stage of sleep, but some more recent evidence suggests that such bed-wetting can also occur at other stages. Sleepwalking also tends to occur most often during the deep sleep of this stage.

As we get older, we sleep more lightly and get less deep sleep. Aging is also linked to shorter time spans of sleep.

B) RAPID EYE MOVEMENT (REM), ALSO KNOWN AS ACTIVE SLEEP OR PARADOXICAL SLEEP

During REM sleep:

- The brain becomes more active.
- The body becomes relaxed and immobilized.

- Dreams occur.
- Eyes move rapidly.

Most dreaming occurs during this stage of sleep, known as rapid eye movement (REM) sleep. REM sleep is characterized by eye movement, increased respiration rate, and increased brain activity.

REM sleep is also referred to as paradoxical sleep because while the brain and other body systems become more active, muscles become more relaxed. Dreaming occurs due to increased brain activity, but voluntary muscles become immobilized.

As the brain begins to relax and slow down, slower waves known as alpha waves are produced. During this time when we are not quite asleep, we may experience strange and extremely vivid sensations known as hypnagogic hallucinations. Common examples of this phenomenon include feeling like we are falling or hearing someone calling our name.

Another very common event during this period is known as a myoclonic jerk. If we have ever startled suddenly for seemingly no reason at all, then we have experienced this phenomenon. While it might seem unusual, these myoclonic jerks are actually quite common.

Previously, experts divided sleep into five different stages. Fairly recently, however, stages 3 and 4 were combined so that there are now three NREM stages and a REM stage of sleep.

2. SLEEP DISORDERS – INSOMANIA

Risks of Insomnia

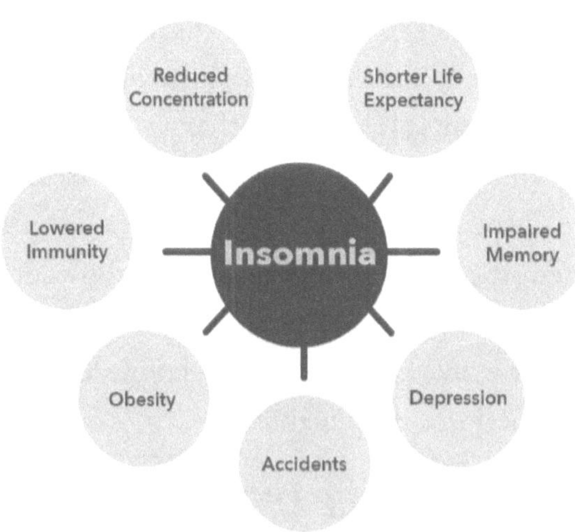

Risk & Effects of Insomania – Sleep Disorders

AN OVERVIEW

Sleep disorders are a group of conditions that affect the ability to sleep well on a regular basis. Whether they are caused by a health problem or by too much stress, sleep disorders are becoming increasingly common world-wide in this modern age.

Most people occasionally experience sleeping problems due to stress, hectic schedules, and other outside influences. However, when these issues begin to occur on a regular basis and interfere with daily life, they may indicate a sleeping disorder.

Depending on the type of sleep disorder, people may have a difficult time falling asleep and may feel extremely tired throughout the day. The lack of sleep can have a negative impact on energy, mood, concentration, and overall health.

In some cases, sleep disorders can be a symptoms of another medical or mental health condition. These sleeping problems may eventually go away once treatment is obtained for the underlying cause. When sleep disorders aren't caused by another condition, treatment normally involves a combination of medical treatments and lifestyle changes.

It's important to receive a diagnosis and treatment right away if we suspect we might have a sleep disorder. When left untreated, the negative effects of sleep disorders can lead to further health consequences. They can also affect our performance at work, cause strain in relationships, and impair our ability to perform daily activities.

SYMPTOMS OF SLEEP DISORDERS

Symptoms can differ depending on the severity and type of sleeping disorder. They may also vary when sleep disorders are a result of another condition. However, general symptoms of sleep disorders include:

- difficulty falling or staying asleep
- daytime fatigue
- strong urge to take naps during the day
- irritability or anxiety
- lack of concentration
- depression

CAUSES OF SLEEP DISORDERS

There are many conditions, diseases, and disorders that can cause sleep disturbances. In many cases, sleep disorders develop as a result of an underlying health problem.

ALLERGIES AND RESPIRATORY PROBLEMS

Allergies, colds, and upper respiratory infections can make it challenging to breathe at night. The inability to breathe through our nose can also cause sleeping difficulties.

NOCTURIA

Nocturia, or frequent urination, may disrupt our sleep by causing us to wake up during the night. Hormonal imbalances and diseases of the urinary tract may contribute to the development of this condition.

CHRONIC PAIN

Constant pain can make it difficult to fall asleep. It might even wake us up after we fall asleep. Some of the most common causes of chronic pain include:

- arthritis
- chronic fatigue syndrome
- fibromyalgia
- inflammatory bowel disease
- persistent headaches
- continuous lower back pain

In some cases, chronic pain may even be exacerbated by sleep disorders. For instance, doctors believe the development of fibromyalgia might be linked to sleeping problems.

STRESS AND ANXIETY

Stress and anxiety often have a negative impact on sleep quality. It can be difficult for us to fall asleep or to stay asleep. Nightmares, sleep talking, or sleepwalking may also disrupt our sleep.

3. STAGES OF SLEEP

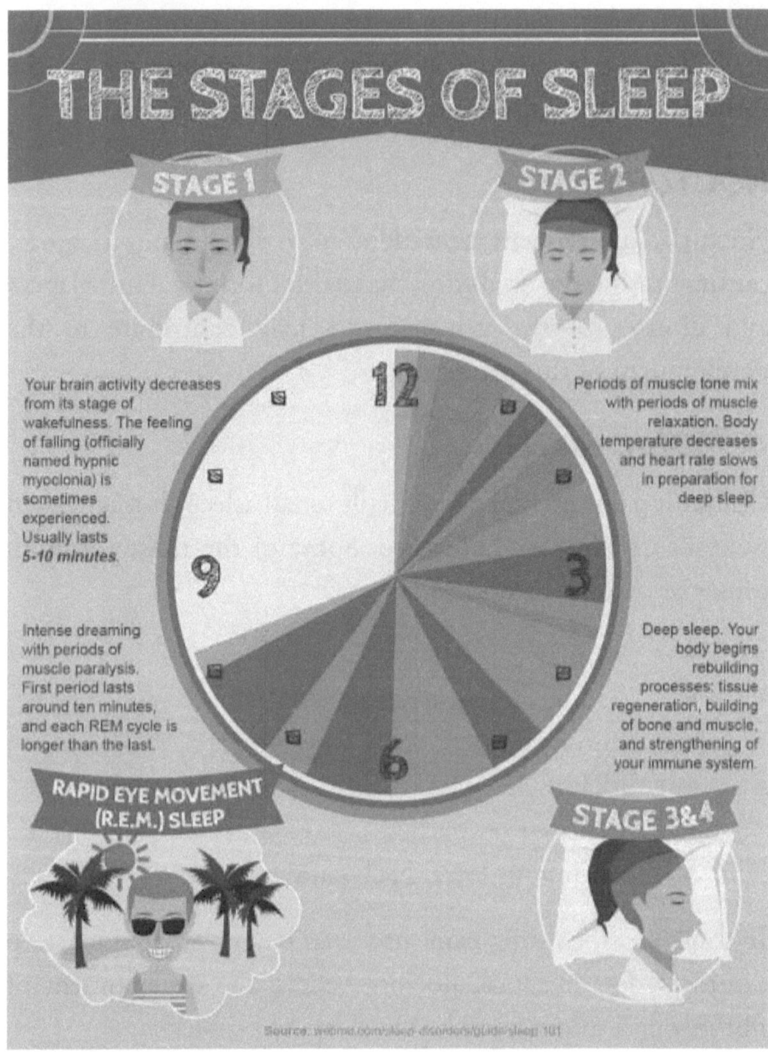

It is important to realize that sleep does not progress through these stages in sequence.

Sleep begins in stage 1 and progresses into stages 2, and 3.

After stage 3 sleep, stage 2 sleep is repeated before entering REM sleep.

Once REM sleep is over, the body usually returns to stage 2 sleep.

Sleep cycles through these stages lasts approximately four or five times throughout the night.

On average, we enter the REM stage approximately 90 minutes after falling asleep.

The first cycle of REM sleep might last only a short amount of time, but each cycle becomes longer. REM sleep can last up to an hour as sleep progresses.

While sleep is often thought of as a passive process, research has shown that the brain is actually quite active during different stages of sleep.

Sleep plays an important role in a number of processes, including memory consolidation and brain clean up.

4. SLEEP CALCULATOR

The ideal amount of sleep varies depending on factors such as age, lifestyle, genetics, and overall health. While there's no universally fixed number of hours that works for everyone, here are some general sleep duration recommendations based on age groups:

Newborns	(0-3 months):	14-17 hours per day
Infants	(4-11 months):	12-15 hours per day
Toddlers	(1-2 years):	11-14 hours per day
Preschoolers	(3-5 years):	10-13 hours per day
School-age Children	(6-13 years):	**9-11 hours per night**
Teenagers	(14-17 years):	**8-10 hours per night**
Adults	(18-64 years):	**7-9 hours per night**
Older Adults	(65+ years):	**7-8 hours per night**

Keep in mind that individual needs can vary. While the recommended ranges are generally helpful, some people might feel their best with slightly more or slightly less sleep. It's important to consider how you feel during the day to determine if you're getting enough rest.

Signs of Getting Enough Sleep:
- Waking up feeling refreshed.
- Maintaining good energy levels throughout the day.
- Being able to concentrate and focus effectively.
- Not experiencing excessive daytime sleepiness or fatigue.

Signs of Not Getting Enough Sleep:
- Feeling excessively tired during the day.
- Struggling to concentrate and stay alert.

- Mood changes, irritability, or mood swings.
- Impaired performance in daily tasks.

Ultimately, the ideal sleep duration for us is the amount that leaves us feeling rested, alert, and able to perform daily activities effectively. If we consistently experience sleep problems or feel we are not getting enough restful sleep, consider consulting a healthcare professional or a sleep specialist. They can help to identify any underlying issues and provide guidance on improving our sleep patterns and overall sleep quality.

IDEAL BEDTIME SLEEP CALCULATOR

This formula tackles sleep quantity. The only information we need is our wake-up time. Here's how it works:

- The average sleep cycle is 90 minutes long
- A typical night of sleep includes 5 full sleep cycles
- 90 x 5 = 450 minutes, or 7.5 hours
- Starting at our wake time, work back 7.5 hours to find our bedtime

For example: We need to wake at 6 a.m. to get ready for work. Counting back 7.5 hours, our ideal bedtime is 10:30 p.m. That means lights out, in bed, ready for sleep at that time.

This bedtime is a starting point, and may need some adjustment, as individual sleep cycles vary in their duration. Try this new bedtime for a week. The goal is to wake naturally about 5-10 minutes ahead of our alarm. If we find ourself waking significantly ahead of our alarm, move our bedtime slightly later. If after a week, we are still sleeping right through to our alarm we need to shift our bedtime earlier. So, adjusting in 15-minute increments until we are waking naturally just before our alarm may result in an optimal and effective sleep hours.

NOT JUST MORE SLEEP, BUT BETTER SLEEP

The *Ideal Bedtime* sleep calculator takes care of sleep quantity. But what about sleep quality? Sleep quality is achieved by sustained rest, with sufficient time spent in each of the four sleep stages—Stages 1-3 and REM sleep—to maintain physical and mental health and function.

SLEEP EFFICIENCY CALCULATOR

Sleep efficiency is one important measure of sleep quality used by sleep scientists and physicians. There's an easy, low-tech way to measure sleep efficiency that requires no sleep tracking devices or equipment. We need only a few basic pieces of information about our night of sleep:

- The total amount of time we spend in bed sleeping – or trying to sleep – between bedtime and waking
- How long it takes us to fall asleep
- The amount of time we spent awake during the night

Let's say we spent a total of 7 hours, or 420 minutes, in bed last night.

It took us 25 minutes to fall asleep.

We spent another 25 minutes awake throughout the night, a result of three separate periods of wakefulness.

Here's how to calculate our sleep efficiency for this night:

- Total sleep time: 420 minutes
- Minus time to fall asleep: 25 minutes
- Minus total time spent awake: 25 minutes
- Actual time spent sleeping: 370 minutes (6 hours, 10 minutes)

Divide 370 minutes by 420 minutes and multiply it by 100 to get the actual percentage value, which is equal to 88%. This number represents your sleep efficiency for that night.

FORMULA FOR CALCULATING SLEEP EFFICIENCY

Sleep Efficiency = (Total Time Asleep / Total Time in Bed) × 100

1. **Total Time Asleep:** This is the total duration of time you spend sleeping during the night. It's the sum of all the time periods you're actually asleep, from the moment you fall asleep until you wake up in the morning.
2. **Total Time in Bed:** This is the total duration of time you spend in bed attempting to sleep, including the time it takes you to fall asleep, any awakenings during the night, and the time you wake up in the morning.

For example, let's say you spent 7 hours and 30 minutes asleep and you were in bed for 8 hours:

Total Time Asleep = 7.5 hours & Total Time in Bed = 8 hours

Sleep Efficiency = (7.5 / 8) × 100 = 93.75%

In this example, your sleep efficiency would be approximately 93.75%.

Interpretation:

- A sleep efficiency of 85% or higher is generally considered good. Ninety percent is considered a very good sleep efficiency.
- Below 85% might indicate that you're spending a significant amount of time in bed awake, which could be due to various factors like frequent awakenings, insomnia, or other sleep disturbances.

Keep in mind that sleep efficiency is just one aspect of sleep quality. If you find that your sleep efficiency is consistently low and you're experiencing sleep difficulties, it's a good idea to consult a healthcare professional or a sleep specialist. They can help you identify the underlying causes and provide guidance on improving your sleep patterns and overall sleep quality.

sanskaaram
The Relevance of
Vedic Science
in Hinduism
A Scientific Approach to
"Rituals"
The ABR Concept
(Act, Belief & Relevance)
CONCEPTUALIZED BY:
Ar. K. SHIVKUMAR

pranoyugam
A Wellness and Well-being
Experiment Based on Vedic Principles
PUSHPANJALI - The Spiritual Intense Mantra
DHAYANAM - The Self Productive Mantra
PRANAYOGAM - The Anti-Stress Mantra
The '3' Pillars of Life
Spiritual, Mental & Physical
CONCEPTUALIZED BY:
Ar. K. SHIVKUMAR

saptamsidhi
A Vedic Approach to Modern Lifestyle
'A Holistic Concept'
आत्मदीपो भव:
[Be Your Own Light]
CONCEPTUALIZED BY:
Ar. K. SHIVKUMAR

saptagyanam
An Overview of the Universal
Cosmic Energy Effect and its
Implications on Human Existence
An Approach To
"PGR" Measures
(Preventive, Guiding & Remedial)
CONCEPTUALIZED BY:
Ar. K. SHIVKUMAR

aarogyaveda
The Vedic and Contemporary
Holistic Health Approach
for Lifestyle Disorders
An Evaluation of
"PST" Measures
(Prevention, Screening & Treatment)
CONCEPTUALIZED BY:
Ar. K. SHIVKUMAR